For Savannah, Sasha and Larichia.

Gail Louw

PLAYS TWO

OBERON BOOKS
LONDON

WWW.OBERONBOOKS.COM

First published in 2018 by Oberon Books Ltd
521 Caledonian Road, London N7 9RH
Tel: +44 (0) 20 7607 3637 / Fax: +44 (0) 20 7607 3629
e-mail: info@oberonbooks.com
www.oberonbooks.com

A catalogue record for this book is available from the British Library.

PB ISBN: 9781786824158
E ISBN: 9781786824165

Cover artwork by Leon Kreel ARPS

Photo of Heather Long in *The Mitfords*

Dress by Hortance Louw (HortamceLouw@gmail.com)

Printed and bound by 4EDGE Limited, Hockley, Essex, UK.
eBook conversion by CPI Group (UK) Ltd, Croydon, CR0 4YY.

Contents

Joe Ho Ho   1

Duwayne   63

The Half Life of Love   109

The Mitfords   167

In Memory of Tony Milner (1947-2015)

JOE HO HO

Characters

LINDA SPARROW, 40

BERYL SPARROW, 70

JOE, 35 – 40

SAHID KHAN, 40

The play takes place in LINDA and BERYL's flat.

Jo Ho Ho was first performed at Devonshire Park Theatre Eastbourne 5 June 2010

Linda	Moira Brooker
Beryl	Kate Dyson
Joe	Jason Pitts
Sahid	Quill Roberts

Producer New Vic Production
Director Tony Milner
Production Manager Paul Debreczeny
Stage Manager Jeremy Barnaby

Act One

In darkness, we hear music and JOE and LINDA murmuring.

JOE: Linda, Linda

LINDA: Oh Joe, Joe!

JOE: Linda, Linda!

LINDA: Nobody's ever kissed me the way you do.

JOE: Linda, Linda!

BERYL: *(Calling.)* Linda, Linda!

> *BERYL's calling suddenly becomes much louder than JOE's murmuring. LINDA comes out of the bedroom door and, switches on the light and reveals BERYL looking at the sofa with her knickers round her ankles.*

BERYL: Linda. I can't find the chain.

LINDA: Mum!

BERYL: It was here earlier.

LINDA: Oh God!

BERYL: Ugh. That's horrible, Linda. Is that mine? Why doesn't this toilet have a hole?

> *LINDA takes off her knickers and walks her to the bathroom off stage. On the way she says*

BERYL: Is it morning? Do I have to go back to bed? I'm hungry. I want my breakfast

LINDA: Mum! You know where the toilet is!

> *LINDA comes back in to the lounge with plastic gloves, a bucket and a toilet roll. She cleans up with her back to the audience. JOE enters and starts caressing and nibbling her. She pushes him away, rather irritated. As she is cleaning BERYL speaks.*

BERYL: What shall I do now, Linda? Shall I wait for you? Shall I come there?

LINDA: Stop it, Joe. Leave me to clean up this disgusting bloody…

JOE: You look so, sexy, in those pink lurex, hmm, come here…

BERYL: Linda, where are you? Are you there? Linda, Linda *(Panicking.)* Linda! Linda!

LINDA: I'm here, Mum!

BERYL walks in.

BERYL: Are you cross with me, Linda? Are you? Are you?

LINDA continues cleaning.

LINDA: How am I going to get you to remember

BERYL: Remember what, dear?

LINDA: Remember which is the toilet and which is the sofa.

BERYL: Why do you say that, Linda? I know the difference. What a funny girl you are.

LINDA: Hmm! *(Pause.)* Come on, let's get you back to bed.

BERYL: No, I don't think so.

LINDA: Well, I think you should.

BERYL: If you want me to, dear.

They move out to the bedroom.

LINDA: I'll be in the lounge. You call if you need me.

BERYL: Thank you dear. You are sweet Linda. You are my sweet girl.

LINDA: Yes mum.

She returns and sits down. JOE is sorting out the records.

LINDA: Do you think I'll make it? Without going mad, I mean.

JOE: Let someone else do it. Someone who's paid to do it. You'll end up nuts. Then who'll love you?

LINDA: I don't care about love.

JOE: Just get rid of her.

LINDA: I can't get rid of her!

JOE: If it was the other way round, she wouldn't've hesitated. Trust me. I know. You should have done it years ago. What

were you waiting for? What were you trying to prove?
That you're a good daughter?

LINDA: Oh stop it.

JOE: That you're good at something.

LINDA: It's not helping!

> *LINDA puts on some music and tidies up. JOE comes and pulls her for a quick step. She starts to laugh and relax.*
>
> *BERYL suddenly screams and rushes in.*

LINDA: Mum. What's the matter? What happened?

BERYL: I don't want to be in the cupboard in the dark.

LINDA: But you're not in a cupboard. You're at home. You're in your own home.

BERYL: Am I not in the cupboard?

LINDA: No. You're at home.

BERYL: But how can I get out of the cupboard?

LINDA: You're not in the cupboard. Look, here's your sofa, and your table. See, it's not a cupboard.

BERYL: But why did you put me in the cupboard?

LINDA: I didn't. You weren't in a cupboard.

BERYL: It was your fault.

LINDA: What was my fault?

BERYL: I wouldn't have done it if it wasn't for you.

LINDA: What wouldn't you have done?

BERYL: I wouldn't've... taken the biscuits. I didn't mean to take them. It wasn't my fault. I hate him!

LINDA: Who do you hate?

BERYL: I just wanted one biscuit. I didn't mean to take them all.

LINDA: You can have all the biscuits you want.

BERYL: But that man

LINDA: Which man?

BERYL: That man, which man, it must have been ...daddy said they might kill me.

7

LINDA: Oh darling! I'm sure he didn't mean it.

BERYL: You always stick up for him. He said he'd kill me.

LINDA: I don't mean to stick up for him.

BERYL: But you do. You always do.

LINDA: I won't anymore. I don't even know him.

BERYL: But he's daddy.

LINDA: Horrible daddy.

BERYL: Yes.

LINDA: Horrible nasty daddy, putting you in the cupboard.

BERYL: But it was you... *(Cries.)*

LINDA: But, don't worry. You won't go into the cupboard again.

BERYL: It's so dark and those bars... I don't want to go to school tomorrow. Do I have to?

LINDA: No. You can stay at home. You don't have to go to school ever again.

BERYL: But then I won't pass my exams.

LINDA: Well, well, then you can go to school.

BERYL: But not tomorrow.

LINDA: No. Not tomorrow. Tomorrow you can stay at home.

BERYL: With you, mummy.

LINDA: Yes. Come to bed now. Come, I'll tuck you up in your nice duvet.

BERYL: What's that?

LINDA: Your blankets. Your nice blankets.

They start to walk away.

BERYL: I thought you'd forgotten me, Linda.

LINDA: How could I do that?

BERYL: Well you have forgotten me before!

JOE makes a rude gesture at BERYL and moves out of the way. He waits near the bedroom watching LINDA.

LINDA: No! I haven't. When did I forget you? Anyway you wouldn't let me forget you, would you! You'd call quick enough!

BERYL: No, I remember that time…

LINDA: What time?

BERYL: Once, when you left me and I called and you didn't come.

She stops and suddenly looks very angry.

LINDA: Come on mum. What's the matter now?

BERYL doesn't respond.

LINDA: Don't worry about it, being, feeling like this at night. Everything's different at night. Everybody gets confused at night, when it's dark and horrible and stuff.

BERYL still doesn't respond.

LINDA: Aren't you talking to me?

JOE: She's sulking.

LINDA: Why are you so cross?

JOE: She doesn't need a reason. She just wants your attention. She's such a child. She always was and now she's ten times worse. Oh come on, if she wants to be like that, let's just go into the bedroom until she starts to behave.

LINDA: What's the matter, mum? Aren't you going to talk to me? What have I done?

JOE: You've done nothing. Come on. I know what you need. And I'm ready for it too. Look at me. Can you see?

LINDA: Aren't you going to talk to me?

JOE: Don't worry about her. Come on. Just a quickie…

BERYL: Hmm.

LINDA: What do you mean, hmm? What's the matter?

BERYL: We never do it anymore.

LINDA: What don't we do anymore?

BERYL: I don't know why you don't want to do it anymore.

LINDA: Do what anymore!

BERYL: Have intercourse.

LINDA: Mum. I'm your daughter!

BERYL: Yes. That's what you always say!

JOE bursts out laughing but tries to stifle it. LINDA goes over to him visibly shocked and upset.

LINDA: My god! That's horrible!

He carries on laughing and she starts to laugh a little as well.

LINDA: Ughh!

She turns back to BERYL.

LINDA: Look, don't worry about that now. You know what, tomorrow, well today is, don't you?

BERYL: What?

LINDA: It's Sunday. And you know what Sunday is, don't you?

BERYL: What am I doing today, Linda?

LINDA: It's Sunday.

BERYL: Is it?

LINDA: Yes. So that means you're going to church.

BERYL: Am I?

LINDA: Yes. You're going with Susan Prosser.

BERYL: But I don't like Susan Prosser.

LINDA: Yes you do. She's your best friend.

BERYL: No she isn't.

LINDA: Who is then?

BERYL: It's that other woman.

LINDA: Which one?

BERYL: That woman with the brown coat.

LINDA: And the handbag and hat?

BERYL: Yes.

LINDA: That's Susan Prosser.

BERYL: Yes. She's my best friend.

LINDA: Well, she's taking you to church today.

BERYL: Church?

LINDA: You always like church.

BERYL: Do I?

LINDA: Yes.

BERYL: I don't think I'll go today. I'll go tomorrow.

LINDA: But today is Sunday, and that's when you go to church.

BERYL: No. I don't want to go.

LINDA: But if you don't go, you won't see Father Gregory.

BERYL: I like Father Gregory. He's got a nice bum.

LINDA: That's right. You go and see Father Gregory's bum.

BERYL: Yes.

LINDA: That'll be nice for you.

BERYL: Goody!

They both laugh and move out to the bedroom.

Fade.

SCENE 2

It is a few days later, in the morning. BERYL is standing at the open front door. She has a big black plastic bag filled with things tied round a walking stick. She is black with rage. LINDA is standing together at a distance from her, watching her expectantly. JOE is with her, standing and watching.

JOE: What is that mad cow going to do now?

LINDA: I don't know what the matter is.

JOE: Did you say something to her?

LINDA: Nothing! But she hardly slept last night. I heard her pacing the flat all night like a bloody lioness. *(Tentatively.)* Mum? Mum? Shall I get you some breakfast. Some nice, egg. Nice eggy on toast?

BERYL stands absolutely still staring out the door.

LINDA: Hmm? What do you think, mum? Some nice, eggy stuff…

BERYL: I know what you're doing.

LINDA: What?

BERYL: You're trying to poison me. You think I'm so stupid, that I'll fall for it. But I won't. See, look at me. I won't!

LINDA: *(To JOE.)* My god. Do you hear that? What the hell's going on? She's never been like this before.

JOE: Phone the cops.

LINDA: Don't be ridiculous.

JOE: Phone the, what they called, social services.

LINDA: I don't know their phone number and she's standing by … let me try.

LINDA walks towards the phone which is near BERYL but as she approaches BERYL turns round on her with the stick as if she is about to beat her and LINDA quickly rushes back to the relative safety of JOE.

BERYL: I want to speak to Simon.

LINDA: But he's dead mum. You know he died when I was little.

BERYL: You can't keep me from speaking to my own husband.

LINDA: But he's dead!

BERYL: Lying to me, poisoning me. *(She opens the front door and screams loudly.)* Help! Help! Somebody help me!

LINDA: Mum for goodness sake! What will the neighbours think!

BERYL: Help! Help! Help me, somebody!

LINDA rushes to the door and slams it, locking it and taking the key. She rushes back to JOE.

BERYL: Yes. Keep me a prisoner. Do your vile dirty deeds on me. But you can't make me eat. So your plans will fail. See, ha ha ha. I'm laughing. I'm laughing at you.

LINDA: I'm not trying to poison you, mum.

BERYL: I'm going to phone Brenda. I'm going to phone Brenda and tell her my own daughter is trying to poison me. I want to speak to Brenda.

LINDA: It's the middle of the night there, mum, in America.

BERYL: You see. Everything I want, you stop. I want to speak to my sister!

LINDA grabs the phone and dials it. After a while there is an answer.

LINDA: Hello Aunty Brenda. Yes, I'm sorry it's so late, early. It's mum, she's, well, she wants to speak to you.

She hands the phone to BERYL.

BERYL: *(Very quietly.)* Brenda. She's trying to kill me. She's poisoning me…… She is! How do you know? I don't know what to do. I tried to escape but the bitch took the key, locked me in. Now there's nowhere to go. I'm going to die. And Simon isn't coming. He went out this morning and left me, just left me. He got out you see. He knew what was happening. Oh my God, what am I going to do? …… But if I go to bed she'll be able to, do anything…… yes. That's it, I'll lock the door. …. Ok. So, I'll wait and then you'll come… I'll lie on the bed but I won't sleep, and you'll be here very soon. An hour? How long's an hour? Just a few moments. Ok. How am I going to get to the room without her getting me? Yes, good idea, ok, see you in a ….

BERYL drops the phone and runs to her bedroom (offstage). LINDA picks up the phone.

LINDA: Well done, Aunty Brenda. All she needs is to get to sleep. Thank you so much… Yes, I'll phone later, let you know. Bye. And sorry.

LINDA rushes into JOE's arms. He sways with her, hums a little melody and they dance together gently and slowly.

SCENE 3

It is two days later. There is a knock at the front door. LINDA has been woken by the knock and comes out of her room in a dressing gown and dashes to the front door. BERYL is sitting at the dining room table eating cereal out of a packet. Milk is spilt on the table and her mouth is like a child's spread with breakfast detritus. LINDA opens the door and SAHID is standing there.

SAHID: Oh, I'm so sorry. It is, were you not, uhm, this is the right…

LINDA: Uhh, sorry?

SAHID: This is 78 Willow Drive, isn't it? I'm so sorry, I might have…

LINDA: Yes. 78 that's right. Willow Drive. People often make mistakes with Road, and Crescent around here… But, sorry, who are you?

SAHID: My name is Mr Khan. Sahid Khan. I, are you, Ms Sparrow? Ms Linda Sparrow?

LINDA: Yes.

SAHID: I left a message on your answerphone. Perhaps you didn't… it was yesterday. I said, you know, if I didn't hear back, I'd, well, I'd assume it was ok. To come see you. You know?

LINDA: Come see me? What about?

SAHID: I just wanted to have a little chat with you.

LINDA: Really, a chat? What about?

SAHID: Ahh, uhm, it was on the answerphone…

LINDA: Oh, I don't think I listened. Hold on a sec, come in, if you want…

She goes to the answerphone and puts it on. SAHID tentatively comes just inside the flat. We hear the answerphone and SAHID interjects as it is on.

ANSWERPHONE: Hello, Ms Sparrow. This is Mr Khan from Social Services. I wonder if it would be alright for me to come and have a little chat with you. Nothing too serious but I would like to come and see you as a matter of urgency so I will come tomorrow at 9.30am. If that is not alright, please call me on 855684. Thank you.

SAHID: Yes, that's the one. You see, it's because I live so close, I thought it would be easy to just pop in on my way to work, you know.

LINDA: Yes I can understand that. So, yes, so you're here. Look I'm really sorry, but I must just, come in, where did you say you're from?

SAHID: Social services.

LINDA: Social services? Oh god, I can't think without a coffee. It's so early.

SAHID: Yes that's because I live…

LINDA: so close, of course. I'll be back, ahm, a coffee, yes? Would you like, milk

SAHID: No, I'm fine thank you, I've just had

LINDA: I won't be…just take a seat… ahm, back in a minute

She exits in the direction of the bathroom

He takes in BERYL for the first time. He is quite surprised at what he sees. She is quite suspicious and doesn't understand what a stranger is doing in the house.

SAHID: Good morning. Are you having your breakfast?

BERYL just looks at him in a very non committal way and continues eating.

SAHID: Would you like a bowl to eat that from?

BERYL: Mind your own bloody business.

SAHID: Oh, I'm sorry.

He moves away as if stung.

BERYL: Linda! Linda! There's a man here. What's he want? What's he doing?

SAHID: Don't worry Mrs Sparrow. I'm sorry I'm interrupting your breakfast. I've only come for a short visit. I'll, I'll be gone very soon.

BERYL: *(Desperate.)* Linda!

LINDA enters.

LINDA: What's the matter, mum?

BERYL: There's a man here.

LINDA: That's alright. This is Mr Khan. *(To him.)* Is it? He's from Social Services. He's not going to do anything to you.

BERYL: What's he here for then?

LINDA: I don't know.

BERYL: What are you here for?

SAHID: I just wanted a little chat with your daughter.

LINDA: You see, he's fine. I'll be back in a mo…

She exits.

BERYL: What do you want to speak to my daughter for?

SAHID: Just a little chat.

BERYL: *(Conspiratorially.)* Is it about......

She stops and SAHID waits for her to carry on.

SAHID: About what?

BERYL: About him?

SAHID: Sorry?

BERYL: About, him?

SAHID: I'm not sure who you mean.

BERYL: Are you from the jail?

SAHID: No. I'm from Social Services.

BERYL: Have you come to, investigate?

SAHID: Yes.

BERYL: *(Shocked.)* Oh, my goodness. Oh my goodness me.

SAHID: There's no need to worry, honestly.

BERYL: She didn't do it, you see. It was an accident.

SAHID: What was?

LINDA returns dressed and with the coffee.

LINDA: Mum? Are you alright, Mr, Khan? Here's some coffee. Oh no, you said you didn't want...

SAHID: That's alright. I'll have it anyway, thanks.

LINDA: *(To BERYL.)* Let's just clean you up a bit, hey.

She wipes her with a kitchen towel and pours some cereal in a bowl, adds milk and BERYL eats happily.

LINDA: *(to SAHID.)* Are you alright? You look, spooked!

SAHID: Sorry! Yes, of course. I suppose she doesn't quite know what she's, saying.

LINDA: Unbelievable what she comes out with! Shall we sit down.

They sit.

SAHID: I'm sorry it's so early.

LINDA: Yes, you said. The chat?

SAHID: Well, we've had, not a complaint exactly but, people are concerned…

LINDA: People, what do you mean?

SAHID: Well there've been comments, not complaints, but people, your neighbours are worried

LINDA: What about? Who's worried?

SAHID: It's about your mother.

LINDA: She's alright. Just a bit confused. She's fine!

SAHID: It's very difficult when someone starts needing support and

LINDA: Support? Who needs support?

SAHID: Well, you might, for example.

LINDA: Me? I'm fine!

SAHID: There's been this shouting in the night and a couple of mornings ago. The neighbours were worried, concerned.

LINDA: Look, she gets a bit upset sometimes. That's no reason…

SAHID: They're just concerned for you.

LINDA: Just tell them…

SAHID: We can offer support. A care package.

LINDA: I can care for her.

SAHID: Of course, but this care package will help you, give you some time off.

LINDA: What will I do with time off?

SAHID: You could do things for yourself. Go out a bit more, get a job.

LINDA: I've got a job. It's called being responsible for my mother. Looking after her, properly, as only I know how to do. That's my job. I think it's time you went. Thank you Mr Khan, for your chat. Maybe you can tell my neighbours to mind their own business.

SAHID: Ms Sparrow, you are being, perhaps, a little, unreasonable.

LINDA: I don't think so. Good-bye.

SAHID: Please contact me if you would like to. Perhaps you wouldn't mind if I popped in again soon, just to see how you are, you know I live very...

LINDA: Close. I know.

SAHID: Good-bye Mrs Sparrow.

SAHID exits.

BERYL: Who was that nice man, Linda?

LINDA: That was a man who wanted to, help us.

BERYL: Help us with what?

LINDA: With looking after us.

BERYL: Do we need looking after, Linda?

LINDA: Mum. I'll be back in a minute. You just keep eating and I'll be back ok! Joe? Joe? Where are you?

Fade.

SCENE 4

It is Sunday morning about two weeks later. LINDA puts down the phone.

LINDA: Mum. That was Susan Prosser.

BERYL: Who?

LINDA: Susan Prosser is coming now.

BERYL: That's nice.

LINDA: To take you to church.

BERYL: Why?

LINDA: Because it's Sunday.

BERYL: Is it?

LINDA: So hurry.

BERYL: Who's coming?

LINDA: Susan Prosser.

BERYL: Who?

LINDA: Your friend Susan Prosser.

BERYL: But I don't think I know anyone called that. Sue who?

LINDA: Not Sue Who. Susan Prosser. Your friend. Your best friend.

BERYL: She's not my best friend.

LINDA: Who is then?

BERYL: Someone else.

LINDA: Someone who wears a brown coat?

BERYL: Yes.

LINDA: And has a handbag and hat?

BERYL: That's the one.

LINDA: You're playing a game, aren't you? Who is it that's going nuts, you or me?

JOE appears.

JOE: It's you, baby.

LINDA: Mmm.

BERYL: I think I'll go back to bed.

LINDA: You're going to church, mum.

BERYL: Do I want to?

JOE: No, we want you out the fucking house, you old fucker.

LINDA: Yes, mum. You want to go to church, because you want to see Father Gregory.

BERYL: He's got a nice bum.

LINDA: That's right.

BERYL: But you know what, Linda.

LINDA: What?

BERYL: He only likes young boys!

JOE: Didn't I always know it!

LINDA: Mum! You can't go around saying things like that!

BERYL: *(Laughing.)* He only likes young boys! He only likes young boys!

BERYL prances off back to her bedroom.

LINDA: *(Laughing.)* Come on Mum. Mrs Prosser might be waiting

She opens the door as she says this and SAHID falls in. He was about to stick a little charity envelope through the door.

SAHID: Oh my goodness. Oh my goodness gracious me. Oh dear

LINDA: What the hell is… who are … oh, it's you. What the hell are you doing?

SAHID: I'm so sorry. It's for the Alzheimer Society, you see. Envelopes for the Alzheimer's Society.

LINDA: You're putting, oh, for goodness' sake, look at that timing *(Starts to laugh.)* how about that for timing, hey! So you're not stalking me?

SAHID: My dear lady, I most certainly am not!

LINDA: No, of course you're not. I'm not being serious. Are you alright? You haven't hurt yourself or anything.

SAHID: No, just a bit. It's never happened before! *(Giggles a little.)* Just at that moment! I'm sorry. You must have got a fright. No, I'm certainly not stalking you.

LINDA: That was a joke. Honest. Well, thanks for the envelope. Here, I can put a couple of pounds in it now and you can take it. Saves you coming back. Is this what you do in your spare time?

SAHID: Well…

LINDA: It's a good thing, community thing. Alzheimer's, good cause.

SAHID: Unfortunately, I have time on my hands now. So, it's, something to do. And you?

LINDA: Me what?

SAHID: Do you have, time on your … no I suppose not.

LINDA: Yes, I'm going shopping, later…

SAHID: And your mother?

LINDA: What about her?

SAHID: Is it alright to leave her alone?

LINDA: As it happens, she's going to church.

SAHID: It sounds like, but, I really wasn't prying.

LINDA: It's alright. I know you people have jobs to do.

SAHID: No, I can assure you. I'm not on duty. But I am a neighbour, you know, I live very close.

LINDA: Yes. You said.

SAHID: I'm repeating myself. I'm sorry.

LINDA: Don't. There's no need…

SAHID: I'm not apologising.

LINDA: No, of course, no need.

SAHID: I was just, this is my neighbourhood.

LINDA: Of course.

SAHID: I didn't mean to imply

LINDA: I didn't assume…

SAHID: It is a nice day. Isn't it?

LINDA: Yes. It is nice.

SAHID: Sometimes it's nice to see someone one knows. Bump into them, or at least, fall through their letterbox! *(LINDA laughs.)* And on a Sunday. Sundays, you know.

LINDA: Sunday bloody Sunday.

SAHID: Do you find that?

LINDA: Sunday bloody Sunday? Nah, it's alright.

SAHID: Some people love Sundays. I used to like it.

LINDA: Sundays. Hmm.

SAHID: I used to like it when I wasn't alone.

LINDA: *(She suddenly looks at him.)*

SAHID: *(Shrugs his shoulders, and can't help looking sorry for himself.)*

LINDA: Hmm.

SAHID: *(Makes more shrugging movements with his hands.)*

LINDA: Alone?

SAHID: It's not so bad.

LINDA: Course not. Answerable to yourself. Free. My God. What I would give… no I don't mean that.

SAHID: At least someone needs you.

LINDA: It doesn't matter who it is, really.

SAHID: As long as it is warm and alive.

LINDA: Even a dog.

SAHID: That's right. Or a cat.

LINDA: It doesn't matter. Dog, cat. It's a living being. You gotta be needed. Haven't you?

SAHID: *(Nods.)*

LINDA: It's not only my mum that needs me. I have others.

SAHID: What? Friends? Children?

LINDA: Others. Anyway, it doesn't matter. Now, you look after yourself, you hear. It's no good going round falling into neighbours' houses, letting any old stranger know you're lonely.

SAHID: You reckon I should just smile

LINDA: Keep a happy face.

SAHID: Smile and the world smiles with you.

LINDA: Happy chappy, not miserable bugger.

SAHID: Yes. No miserable buggers.

LINDA: We're all happy chappies.

SAHID: Not miserable buggers.

LINDA: Bye bye, happy chappy.

SAHID: Bye bye. Happy chappy.

   SAHID walks off. BERYL walks in with her hat.

BERYL: You mustn't talk to strangers, Linda. I've always told you.

LINDA: He's not a stranger. He was in our house.

BERYL: Who was in our house? Was a stranger in our house?

LINDA: No. This social worker bloke.

BERYL: Why was he in our house?

LINDA: He wasn't in our house. Well, vaguely in, just outside.

BERYL: But you said

LINDA: I mean he was in our house but not ….

BERYL: I don't like that Susan Prosser.

LINDA: Why not?

BERYL: She tells me what to do. All the time. I'm not a child.

LINDA: When did she tell you what to do?

BERYL: All the time. She keeps telling me to shush in church. I don't want to be shushed. It's insulting. That's what it is. Everyone looks at me. She makes such a noise. Shush. Shush!

LINDA: Oh God.

BERYL: I tell her. Stop shushing. The more I tell her, the more she shushes.

LINDA: Oh my God.

LINDA gets up from the table and busies herself, trying to stop crying. BERYL doesn't notice anything. JOE notices and comes over.

JOE: What's up doll?

LINDA: Oh God, please don't let Susan Prosser give up on my mother. Please let her keep on taking her to church on Sunday. Please God, please.

JOE: Ok, doll!

LINDA: Oh stop it, Joe. You don't understand.

JOE: Course I do. Come on sweetheart. I think I know what you want.

LINDA: No. Leave me alone.

JOE: Come on. I'm the doctor. Doctor's orders. Who knows best? Listen to daddy.

LINDA: You're not the doctor and you're not the daddy.

JOE: I'm God. And God is the doctor and the daddy.

LINDA: Stop blaspheming.

JOE: I am your god.

LINDA: I don't need a god.

JOE: You need this god.

LINDA: No, I …

JOE: Yes, you do. Now come on. Let's get into that bedroom before that old fucker there starts making her filthy demands.

BERYL: Linda?

She turns to her but JOE carries on into the bedroom.

JOE: I'm waiting for you, Linda. Don't keep me waiting.

LINDA: What is it, mum?

There is a sudden knock at the door.

JOE: Who the hell is that? Tell them to fuck off. You're busy …

LINDA: It must be Mrs Prosser.

BERYL: There's someone at the door, Linda.

JOE goes into the bedroom. LINDA goes to the door. SAHID is standing there with a pack in his hands.

SAHID: Am I disturbing? I'm sorry, I just thought, maybe you're interested

LINDA: My God, you are stalking…

SAHID: No, I'm, it's just, the Alzheimer's society, this pack gives you so much information

He tries to hand her the pack.

LINDA: I'm sorry. But, ahm, I'm a bit, busy, really.

BERYL: Who is that man, Linda?

LINDA: It's Mr Khan.

SAHID: Please, Sahid.

LINDA: The man I told you, I mean, the man who was here earlier

BERYL: Which man was here earlier?

LINDA: This man, mum. Mr Khan.

BERYL: I don't like strangers in the house.

LINDA: He's not a stranger.

BERYL: Tell him to go, Linda. Tell him to go! I won't have him in the house. He must go. Tell him to go!

LINDA: *(She suddenly stops.)* Sahid. Come and sit down. Take a seat here.

SAHID: If you're sure *(tentatively, looking at BERYL, but comes in quite pleased.)*

LINDA: Now, Sahid. I'm going to make you a nice cup of tea.

SAHID: That would be very, welcome, Mrs Sparrow.

LINDA: You can call me Linda!

SCENE 5

It is a couple of hours later… LINDA and SAHID are very happy and under the influence of quite a bit of booze. BERYL is at church.

SAHID: You know. I'm a Moslem and I don't drink wine.

LINDA: You know. Somehow I don't believe you!

They both burst out laughing.

SAHID: I'm not a very good Moslem. When I was a student I grew up not drinking. Then I drank. Then I stopped. I tried to be a good Moslem. That it would make my life better. Not drinking was one of those things that irritated Charlotte more than anything.

LINDA: What sort of name is Charlotte anyway? She sounds up her own arse.

SAHID: *(He is shocked but then laughs.)* That's it. Exactly, she is. Up her own arse!

LINDA: As long as she's not up anyone else's.

SAHID: *(He stops laughing and looks crestfallen.)* But that's the problem. She probably is!

He suddenly finds that hilarious too and the two of them laugh.

SAHID: She's very beautiful you know. She was my first love.

LINDA: But you obviously weren't her last…

Again they laugh.

SAHID: Do you know something? I shouldn't say it, we hardly know each other, but, I mean, honestly, I never thought I could live without her.

LINDA: You know what you gotta do? You gotta go out there and find yourself a Claudette, or no, a, a Tracy. That's it, not Charlotte, or Patricia or, or Sienna, or, no you need Tracy, or Shaz, or, or, that's what you gotta do. Trust me.

SAHID: No, you're wrong, not Tracy. I've got to find myself an Aisha.

LINDA: Aisha?

SAHID: They found Aisha. Mother and father. From a good family. Good mother. Good father. Seven brothers.

LINDA: Seven brothers!

SAHID: I would have had seven brothers in law. But I wanted to go to England, to study. An English degree.

LINDA: To study social work.

SAHID: Not at first. You don't go to England to study social work. You go to study medicine, engineering, computing.

LINDA: What did you study?

SAHID: Engineering.

LINDA: So you're an engineer?

SAHID: I was for a few years.

LINDA: And?

SAHID: I hated it. I wanted to work with people, not numbers, maths. I wanted to, no. You'll laugh.

LINDA: No I won't.

SAHID: To do some good.

Obviously LINDA starts laughing but then immediately stops.

LINDA: I think that's, no, really… special.

SAHID: You think it's ridiculous.

LINDA: I don't. So, what happened to Aisha.

SAHID: Did I tell you she had seven brothers? I would have had seven brothers in law. Her parents found someone else for her. Not a social worker.

LINDA: And you found Charlotte…

SAHID: She didn't even have one brother.

LINDA: Did she have a sister?

SAHID: She had a horse.

LINDA: A horse!

SAHID: A horse.

LINDA: A horse is good!

They find this hilarious.

SAHID: It's good to laugh.

LINDA: It's been ages since I've had a really, really

SAHID: I don't always find it easy, to just,

LINDA: No, nor me.

SAHID: I'm really glad I met you, Linda. I noticed you once, you know.

LINDA: You noticed me?

SAHID: In the shops once. I thought, my goodness, that is a good looking lady.

LINDA: What?

SAHID: I couldn't believe it when I saw it was you, when I first came in and saw the lady was you.

LINDA: I...I ...I

SAHID: I thought, my goodness, Sahid. At long last, your luck appears to be in.

LINDA: But...

SAHID: Does it bother you, me saying that?

LINDA: No, of course, I just...

SAHID: I'm sorry. Maybe I was too, presumptive...

LINDA: No, it's alright.

SAHID: It's true. I really looked at you, and my heart, it went...

LINDA: No don't. Please. Can you, get me some water, the kitchen. My head... There's aspirin, it's in the top drawer. Do you mind...

SAHID: No, of course

Exits.

LINDA: Joe.

JOE: What do you want?!

LINDA: I wanted to see you.

JOE: Why?

LINDA: I just, wanted to see you for a minute.

JOE: Oh just piss off.

LINDA: Don't be like that!

JOE: Go on, piss off. Go to that, loser.

LINDA: Why's he a loser?

JOE: He thinks you're pretty! What else is he?

LINDA: How can you be so, mean!

JOE: Why're you coming to me? Huh? Why? All getting a bit too much for you out there? Can't handle it? If you can't cope with hot water, don't get in the bloody bath!

LINDA: What should I do?

JOE: What should you do? Why are you coming to me to ask? Are you such a baby? Little baby. Little fat baby. Little stupid fat baby.

LINDA: I think he's going to, kiss me.

JOE: Let him rape you! I couldn't give a shit!

JOE goes back into the bedroom

SAHID: *(Handing her the water and pills.)* Here you are.

LINDA: *(Distracted.)* I, I'm sorry, I

SAHID: I didn't mean to upset you. But, you are

LINDA: Please, don't.

SAHID: I won't. Not if it upsets you. Come, sit down. We were having... I am stupid sometimes!

LINDA: No. You're not. It's me.

SAHID: Will you sit here?

LINDA sits next to him.

SAHID: Shall we have another drink?

LINDA: I suppose we could.

They both drink. They sit uncomfortably at first and then slowly relax a little.

SAHID: We could, go out together one evening. A meal.

LINDA nods very tentatively.

SAHID: I suppose it's difficult.

LINDA: Yes.

SAHID: Your mother, I mean.

LINDA: Yes of course. I can't leave her.

SAHID: She could come too.

LINDA laughs disparagingly.

LINDA: I'm sorry. But, I don't think that's much of an idea.

SAHID: I'd rather it was just us.

LINDA: You'd really be taking your philanthropy just a little too far.

SAHID: It's good to see you laugh again, Linda.

LINDA: Can you imagine it! My mother in a restaurant. My God!

SAHID: It will be good to go together. Just the two of us. We could really get to know each other, you know.

LINDA: I'm sorry Sahid. I... won't be a moment, just a, sec

She gets up and goes into the bedroom. SAHID looks after her. He is surprised and moves towards the bedroom door trying to listen.

LINDA: Joe! Joe! I... just, Joe! Don't .... Oh come on, Joe. I don't know what to do... ...Joe! Don't be like that!

SAHID hears her about to come out and rushes back and picks up an old LP, as if he's been looking at them.

SAHID: Look at this. Mantovani. My goodness. Is it yours?

LINDA: No. It's my mother's. Old LPs.

SAHID: You don't mind, do you, if I put it on.

LINDA vaguely shakes her head and he puts the record on. LINDA is very distracted.

LINDA: You must go.

SAHID: Pardon?

LINDA: You must go. I can't have you here.

SAHID: Why?

LINDA: It's not right.

SAHID: For whom?

LINDA: For, my mother.

SAHID: Your mother?

LINDA: Yes. She's, not a well woman, you know.

SAHID: She's at church.

LINDA: But when she gets back. She'll come in and, get a terrible fright.

SAHID: Alright Linda.

LINDA: I'm sorry. I just, can't have it.

SAHID: But why?

LINDA: Because…

SAHID: I like you, Linda.

LINDA: That's it, you see. If you didn't show it. You're making it so bloody obvious.

SAHID: Is that a problem?

LINDA: Yes it is.

SAHID: I don't want to lie. I like you. Must I pretend I don't?

LINDA: Yes.

SAHID: I can't Linda. I don't understand why I should.

LINDA: But next minute you're going to, try and kiss me.

SAHID: I could, if you want me to.

LINDA: That's it. I don't. You see, where will it end?

SAHID: Where will it end? There, it, it can end there, if you want it to.

LINDA: It never ends there.

SAHID: We're two adults, Linda.

LINDA: I'm sorry…I've got to… I must…

She starts to leave and he grabs her arm.

SAHID: Where are you going? Why do you have to go?

LINDA: Leave me! I've got to go, I've got to see

SAHID: See who? Who's there? Is there someone there?

LINDA: Nobody, I, it's my, bladder!

SAHID: Don't lie, Linda. Where are you rushing? Why?

She rushes out and runs to her room, slamming the door behind her.

LINDA: Joe. I'm sorry Joe! I'm sorry. Say you'll forgive me, Joe. Oh Joe!

SAHID stands, waiting.

FADE.

SCENE 6

It is next morning. BERYL is eating breakfast and humming something incoherent to herself. LINDA is sitting on the sofa with her head between her legs.

BERYL: I want some more egg, Linda

LINDA: You're not allowed more egg.

BERYL: Linda. Linda. I want some more egg.

LINDA: The doctor says you must be careful of your cholesterol, so you're not allowed more than one egg.

BERYL: But I want another one.

LINDA: But you can't have another one.

BERYL: Yes I can. You're not my mother. Are you?

LINDA: Yes I am. Now be very quiet and don't say another word.

BERYL: Why not?

LINDA: Because I'm asking you to. Because I've got a really bad headache, and I need five minutes, just five minutes of nothing. Please!

BERYL goes out of the room. After a minute or so she comes back with something wrapped in toilet paper. She sits at the table and wraps it up in newspaper. Then takes another piece of paper and wraps it up again.

LINDA staggers up and notices her mother. She looks at her suspiciously.

LINDA: What's that you've got, mum?

BERYL: This dear?

LINDA: Yes. What is it?

BERYL: Oh nothing.

LINDA: Nothing?

BERYL: Just a little something I made.

LINDA: Where did you make it?

BERYL: This?

LINDA: Did you make it in the toilet?

BERYL: Yes, I did, actually.

LINDA: Let me take it from you.

BERYL: No thanks, dear.

LINDA: I think I had better, mum.

BERYL: That's nice of you dear, but I'm fine.

LINDA: Give it to me, mum.

BERYL: No. It's mine!

LINDA: I said, give it to me!

BERYL: No. Shan't, shan't. It's mine. It's mine!

LINDA makes a grab for it and BERYL tries to snatch it back. They fight over it and all of a sudden the turd is thrown on the floor. They both stop and look at it.

BERYL: Now see what's happened. It's lost its pretty package.

They both stand there looking at it and JOE walks in. He looks at it too.

JOE: It's like a cat's dead mouse. Isn't it?

LINDA: A trophy.

JOE: A product of her functioning systems.

LINDA: All's working well.

BERYL: It is very brown. Don't you think, Linda?

LINDA: I must have been very bad in my previous life. Very wicked. Let's make her suffer in this life, God said. Let's make her really suffer.

She gets the newspaper and picks it up and takes it to the toilet and we hear the loo flush. She comes back and cleans the carpet. She speaks all the while.

I mean not just, let's make sure she doesn't have children, or a husband, or a home of her own. No, let's go to town.

Let's really go to town. We'll give her a mother who
poos on the sofa, or who wraps up her poo in paper and
presents it to her. No doesn't present it to her. That would
be just too easy. We'll let her fight with her mother over the
poo, and then it can get thrown onto the carpet. I know,
let's get them to squash it into the carpet and walk all over
the house with poo on their feet. Ok that's just too silly.
We'll let her just pick it up. We'll be kind to her. Poor love,
we can't be that mean, can we.

BERYL: I'm hungry. I want an egg.

JOE: Give the old bat an egg, Linda.

LINDA: *(Screaming.)* She's not allowed an egg. She has high
cholesterol, for Christ's bloody sake!

JOE: Right, so she's going to die from Alzheimer's but with
perfect cholesterol. What the fuck's the difference?!

LINDA: Right! You want an egg? You want six eggs? Fine!

BERYL: I only want one egg, Linda.

LINDA: I'll have the rest. It'll be such a pleasure dying from
high bloody cholesterol. I only wish it didn't take ten years
to happen!

BERYL: Nobody ever let me have more than one egg.

LINDA: Who's nobody? There's only me. There's only ever
me! What do you mean, nobody?

BERYL: Whenever I wanted two eggs when I was

LINDA: little?

BERYL: When I was in that place.

LINDA: What place? What you talking about?

BERYL: When you didn't come and see me.

LINDA: You've always been here! Where else would you have
been?

BERYL: I wasn't always here. I was in that place. You
remember. I was in that place, with those people, you
remember, you remember, Linda!

LINDA: I don't remember anything!

JOE: Why are you behaving like a fool?

LINDA: Don't you start on me!

BERYL: What Linda? What mustn't I do?

JOE: You're being ridiculous.

LINDA: Leave me alone!

BERYL: I'm not touching you, Linda!

JOE: You know she was in that place. You know it. Why are you pretending?

LINDA: I don't know anything!

BERYL: You remember, Linda.

JOE: You say you don't remember. Only a fool doesn't remember. You know where she was. You know why she was there!

LINDA: I don't know anything.

BERYL: But you do, Linda.

JOE: You're going crazy, you mad woman. Look at you. Look at your hair. Look at your hair lying so flat and lanky. Look how horrible you look. Look at you, you're fat, you're ugly.

LINDA: Stop it! Just stop it!

BERYL: Stop what, Linda! What's the matter? You're making me scared.

JOE: You're a nobody, a useless, waste of space. So ugly, so horrible. Nobody could love you. Look at you, you patchy, your nose is like an elephant's. Even your fingernails, look how yellow, how old. You haven't lived.

LINDA: Shut up! Shut up!

JOE: Look what you've become. Why don't you just do something that would really help humankind. Do something sensible for once in your life. I mean, what the fuck are you anyway? Some ridiculous, lousy, useless fuck that just

LINDA: Stop it! Stop it!

JOE: Waste of space, waste of air, of breath. What good are you?

LINDA: I've had enough. I can't take it. I can't live with you. You're driving me mad. I'm going to go crazy. You'll drive me to that place.

BERYL: What place?

LINDA: That place. It wasn't her in that place.

BERYL: What place, Linda?

LINDA: It was *me*! I was there, not her.

BERYL: Really dear?

LINDA: Me! I was there, in that place. Not you.

BERYL: That's nice dear.

LINDA: He's driving me back there.

BERYL: Who, Linda.

LINDA: Him. He's got to go.

BERYL: Well then, you tell him to go.

LINDA: Go. You heard her. Get out of my life.

BERYL: *(To herself.)* Do we have a gardener?

JOE: Linda. Control yourself.

LINDA: I mean it. I won't take it anymore. You have to go.

LINDA grabs a knife and starts going for JOE. BERYL looks slightly anxious and watches LINDA, confused, worried.

JOE: Stop being so ridiculous.

LINDA: Get out of my life. I mean it. Get out!

JOE: I'll leave you, Linda. If I go, that's it. It'll be the end. I won't come back into your life.

LINDA: Go!

JOE: This is your last chance. If I go, I won't be back.

LINDA: Go!

JOE turns on his heel and walks out. LINDA stops. She lets out a little laugh, then the realisation dawns on her slowly.

LINDA: Joe? Where've you gone? You can come back now. Joe? Are you there? I didn't mean it, you know. You know when I'm joking, don't you? For God's sake, can't you take a joke? You used to be able to. You used to know when I was joking! Joe! Where are you? Stop fooling about! Come back. Joe? I can feel you. I know you're there. Come, Joe. Come, come back. Come, let's go into the bedroom. Let's play that game. The game you like. Your favour... Come on! Joe! Come on! Where are you? Joe, please, please.

BERYL: What's the matter, Linda? What are you doing?

LINDA: *(She starts crying.)* He's gone.

BERYL: Who's gone, dear?

LINDA: He's gone.

BERYL: I'm here. There's no-one else.

LINDA: I can't live, just you and me.

BERYL: It's always you and me, dear. It's always been you and me. Hasn't it?

LINDA: I can't, anymore. It's like, last time. I can't, anymore. Joe? Are you there? Are you coming back? I can't live without you, Joe.

LINDA suddenly turns the knife on herself.

BERYL: Linda! What are you doing with that knife? Put it down. Help, somebody help! Linda, stop, stop!

LINDA pushes the knife into her middle. She drops the knife and collapses.

BERYL: Oh no! Linda, Blood! Blood! Oh my God! Linda! Linda what are you doing? What can I do? What must I do? Linda tell me. What must I do?

She rushes out the front door screaming.

BERYL: *(Screaming.)* I didn't do it! It wasn't me! I never touched her! *(Pause.)* What's going to happen to me!

DARK.

Act Two

*It is a month later. LINDA and BERYL walk into their home. LINDA
walks cautiously. She has clearly had surgery in her abdomen and has
spent time recuperating. They take off their coats. SAHID follows behind.
LINDA sits down. She seems resigned. BERYL is very confused, far more
so than before.*

SAHID: There we are. Is it good to be home?

BERYL: Is that where we are?

SAHID: Yes. Is it good? Are you happy?

BERYL: Which room should be mine?

SAHID: It is your room. It's over there, isn't it? Do you want to
    go and see it?

BERYL: Can I?

SAHID: Yes.

    She exits.

SAHID: What are you looking for, Linda? Is there something
    you need? A cup of tea? I'll go put the kettle on. You relax.
    Just use me.

LINDA: I…

SAHID: There's no need to thank me. I want to be here with
    you. You sit down. I'll be back in a moment.

    SAHID brings her a packet of biscuits.

SAHID: I bought some biscuits. Do you like these?

    LINDA takes one and eats it.

SAHID: I like them. Actually, they were Charlotte's favourites.

LINDA: Charlotte, the horse.

SAHID: Yes. Charlotte, the horse.

    LINDA smiles.

SAHID: It's good to see you smile. You haven't smiled this past
    month.

The phone rings. Without thinking SAHID answers it.

SAHID: Hello. I don't know, what number do you want... Yes, that's the right number.... I'm afraid Mrs Sparrow is a little indisposed at the moment. Can I help?... A friend... Mrs Prosser *(He turns and mouths her name to LINDA who remains unresponsive.)* Ahh, yes of course, you are the lady who comes for Mrs Sparrow ... Yes, oh that's excellent. I'm sure she'll be very pleased.... Yes, I'll make sure she's ready. Well, see you later. Goodbye.

(Calling.) Mrs Sparrow.

BERYL: Did I hear someone call me?

SAHID: Yes, it was me.

BERYL: Oh hello. I didn't know you came in. Can I help you?

SAHID: It's me, Mrs Sparrow, remember?

BERYL: Oh yes, I do remember you. It's been such a long time. How are you?

SAHID: I'm, eh, fine. Thanks.

BERYL: Why don't you come and visit me anymore?

SAHID: Ahm, the phone just rang and, do you know who it was?

BERYL: No I don't, dear. Don't you?

SAHID: I mean, it was your friend, Mrs Prosser.

BERYL: Oh, she's not my friend, dear.

SAHID: Well she seemed to think she was.

BERYL: Oh no.

SAHID: But she's coming to fetch you, for church.

BERYL: Oh no. I can't go with her, dear.

SAHID: But she's coming, soon, to take you. She said she'd hoot outside.

BERYL: But I don't know her. I can't go with someone I don't know, can I? That would be very silly.

LINDA is smiling to herself.

SAHID: Well, shall I phone back quickly and tell her you don't want to...

BERYL: Oh I think so, dear.

SAHID: I could do 1471, 3, isn't it?

LINDA: It's Mrs Prosser, mum.

BERYL: But I don't know her.

LINDA: She's the one with the brown coat

BERYL: Brown coat?

LINDA: And bag. She's going to take you to church.

BERYL: But I'm not allowed out. I can go into the lounge.

LINDA: You're not in the home anymore, mum.

BERYL: Which home is that, dear?

LINDA: Would you like to go to church?

BERYL: Ooh yes. If I'm allowed.

LINDA: You'll see Father Gregory.

BERYL: Do I like Father Gregory?

LINDA: Yes. You love Father Gregory. Go and put on your shoes.

BERYL: He's got a nice bum. That's what the woman used to say.

LINDA: Which woman?

BERYL: The one who lived here.

LINDA: That'll be me. Go on, go get your shoes.

BERYL: Which ones?

LINDA: Your Sunday shoes.

BERYL: Oh goody!

BERYL exits and comes back wearing slippers and a coat. No-one notices. There is a hoot outside.

BERYL: Bye bye all of you. So nice of you to drop by. You will come again, won't you?

SAHID walks her to the door and waves while she goes out.

SAHID: I made some soup for you Linda. I bought these excellent vegetables. So nutritious and cooked them all up with some stock. You need building up, you see. I'm going to go and heat it up. You wait here...

He exits.

LINDA sits watching the bedroom door. She is fixed on it, fixated and suddenly, slowly, the door knob turns. She is very relieved. JOE stands in the doorway.

JOE: Whatcha.

LINDA: You came back!

JOE: Course I did. What d'ya think! That I'd leave my girl?

LINDA: You might've.

JOE: Why would I?

LINDA: Because I told you to.

JOE: Well you see, I know you better than you know yourself.

LINDA: That'd be funny....

JOE: Come here, darling. Come and give me a cuddle.

LINDA: *(She gets up slowly, still in some pain. She goes to him in the doorway and they hold each other.)*

JOE: You are a silly billy, aren't you?

LINDA: Don't patronise me.

JOE: What do you go and cause yourself damage?

LINDA: I wanted to hurt you.

JOE: Well you did! I suffered.

LINDA: How did you suffer?

JOE: I missed you. It was lonely all that time you were gone. I spent the whole month waiting for you to come back to me.

LINDA: *(Sarcastic.)* I'm crying for you.

JOE: I'm not asking you to do that. Just understand what it was like for me.

LINDA: What about what it was like for me.

JOE: But you had a wonderful time. You didn't have to do anything. You didn't have to look after her. You didn't have to cook, clean, nothing. Just talk to people about how you were feeling.

LINDA: You don't understand anything.

JOE: I understand that I missed you.

LINDA: Missed sex.

JOE: That I love you.

LINDA: Do you?

JOE: Of course I do.

LINDA: Do you really?

SAHID enters with some fruit. LINDA gets a shock and quickly closes the door.

SAHID: What's the matter?

LINDA: What?

SAHID: I said, what's the matter? You're looking so strange?

LINDA: I'm just, busy that's all.

SAHID: Busy? What're you busy doing?

LINDA: Why do you want to know?

SAHID: I've, brought you some fruit.

LINDA: I don't want fruit. I just want to be, left alone!

SAHID: But you're not well. I'm here to look after you.

LINDA: I don't want you to look after me!

SAHID: The doctor said you could come home, and your mother could come home, only if you had help.

LINDA: You're not my helper.

SAHID: But I'm your friend. Please let me help you.

LINDA just stares at him.

SAHID: I'll just, get the soup

SAHID exits and LINDA opens the door.

JOE: It looks as though you don't need me.

LINDA: Of course I need you. I've needed you since I was sixteen.

JOE: But there's someone else now to look after you.

LINDA: You've always looked after me.

JOE: I have.

LINDA: Always cared for me.

JOE: Yes.

LINDA: You were always there.

JOE: Always there.

LINDA: For me.

JOE: For you.

LINDA: Just for me.

JOE: Yes. Just for you.

They hug.

LINDA: It'll be just like it's always been. Won't it?

JOE: Just like it's always been.

LINDA: I don't need anybody else. Not when I've got you.

JOE: Course not.

LINDA: I'll get rid of him. That bloke out there. That soup maker, fruit bringer. Don't need him. Not with you here.

JOE: No. I'm here. For more important things. What do you need fruit and soup when I've got so much more to offer.

SAHID comes in with soup and puts it on the table. This gives time for LINDA to move away.

SAHID: Here you are. Linda. Come sit down. Come away from the door.

LINDA: But.

SAHID: Come. You don't need to go into the bedroom. There's nothing there for you. Come over here. Come sit down and eat this soup.

LINDA hesitates. The soup smells good.

SAHID: Come on. Away from there. You don't need to go in there.

LINDA: But, ahm, I …

SAHID: Come. Trust me. There's nothing there for you. There's nothing in that room. Come sit here with me and have this soup.

She moves a few steps forward.

SAHID: That's it. Can you smell it? It smells so good, doesn't it? It's good for you. It's nourishing. Thick vegetable soup. Come, come sit. You'll feel better.

She moves further forward.

SAHID: That's it. Nice and comfortable. Here you are.

He feeds her the first mouthful.

LINDA: Mmm.

SAHID: Go on. Have another spoonful. Just one.

She has it.

SAHID: And one more.

She eats it and starts really to enjoy it.

LINDA: This is delicious,

SAHID: I know.

LINDA: I'm really hungry.

SAHID: Eat.

LINDA: How did you make it? Did someone teach you?

SAHID: No. I taught myself.

LINDA laughs gently and carries on eating.

She looks at SAHID.

LINDA: I didn't realise I was so hungry. *(She eats.)* Actually, you're very kind.

SAHID: I'm not doing this to be kind.

LINDA: Why are you doing it?

SAHID: I, well, we're friends, aren't we? I thought we were friends. Friends do this for each other. Look after, look out.

JOE appears in the doorway. LINDA reacts and SAHID notices it. He puts his hand on her arm, to steady her almost.

SAHID: Friends like to see their friends enjoy the food they've made, especially for them.

He watches her and she carries on eating.

JOE: Oh please, do me a favour. I might just be sick in your soup. Friends do this, friends do that. Ooohh, I'm your friend, Linda. Let me cook for you. Yuck!

SAHID: I like to see you eat, Linda. I feel this incredible sense of wanting you to be well, and, healthy.

JOE: Well and healthy. What's he saying? That you're sick, sicko, are you sick you sick sicko sick sick.

SAHID: I feel this, warmth to you, Linda. I have tried to fight it. You seem so, uninterested, but, I can't and I find myself coming back, constantly, unable to stay away.

JOE: Linda! Linda are you listening to this bloke? Have you ever heard such crap in your life, such bullshit. Linda? Are you listening to him?

SAHID: I'm sorry Linda. I know it's not what you want to hear from me. I'll stop, if you want me to.

LINDA: No. You don't have to stop.

SAHID: Does that mean there's, some hope for me?

JOE: No you goddamn arsehole. It doesn't mean that. There's only one person in this world for this woman and that's me. This world ain't big enough for two of us, matey! Ha, Linda, what a fool hey? What a shitty horrible ugly little fool, hey, hey Linda? Hey, hey, Linda, Linda. Tell the shithole to go home, to get out of here. Go on, Linda, tell him. Go on, tell him. We'll go to bed, we'll play that game, that special game. You know the one, the one where the prince comes and kisses the ugly little girl and she turns into a beautiful princess. And all the horrible people around her disappear into nothing and she becomes the queen of them all and takes the handsome prince into her bed and they make love. And we can have a beautiful baby.

LINDA: NO! How dare you! How dare you talk about a baby! I don't have a baby! Go away! I don't want to see you again. I don't want you in my life anymore. Get out of here, get out of my life. I won't have you, anymore. It's finished. It's over. Get out!

JOE: Oh fuck off you, if that's what you want.

LINDA stands up screaming.

LINDA: Yes! That's what I want. Fuck off! Get out!

JOE exits.

LINDA stops. She starts to get up to move to the bedroom. As she does this SAHID gets up too. He grabs her, and holds her fiercely.

LINDA: No leave me, I have to go, go to him…

SAHID: No Linda. Don't go anywhere! Stay. Don't, just stay. Now.

LINDA: *(Struggling to get away.)* You don't understand! He'll go. Joe will go. He'll leave. I have to get there…

SAHID: Let him go, Linda. You don't need him.

SAHID keeps hold of her as she struggles, moaning, until she sobs and gently gives way. She is utterly exhausted and lays her head on his shoulder. He carries her to the sofa and lays her down, covering her with a little blanket that is nearby.

LINDA: *(Whispering.)* Thank you.

She falls asleep.

SAHID is shaken and he looks at the bedroom. He takes a deep breath but is determined and stands looking into the bedroom He puts on the light and looks round to make sure there really is no-one there. He suddenly grabs the bedclothes off the bed and starts stripping off all the sheets, throwing them down vigorously. We see the sheets come flying into the room.

BLACK

SCENE 2

It is several weeks later. LINDA is asleep in bed. We hear BERYL calling, softly then louder and louder.

BERYL: Linda! Linda!

LINDA jumps up out of bed and runs to the lounge. Her mother is sitting on the sofa but her knickers are where they should be. LINDA breathes a sigh of relief. BERYL is wearing a dressing gown.

BERYL: I'm hungry, Linda. I want my breakfast.

LINDA: Oh mum. It's so early. Why do you want to eat so early, oh, it doesn't matter. Here, I'll get you some cereal.

BERYL: I don't want cereal. I want eggs

LINDA: Alright. You can have one egg. You can have a nice piece of toast with it.

BERYL: And marmalade.

LINDA: Yes. And marmalade. *(She smiles at her mother.)* Only the best marmalade.

BERYL: Yes

LINDA: *(Affectionately.)* For Mrs Queen!

BERYL: Who's Mrs Queen.

LINDA: You can be Mrs Queen. The Queen of them all! The loveliest and sweetest of all the women in the world!

BERYL: Is my name Mrs Queen?

LINDA: No. You know your name. Don't you know your name?

BERYL: Of course I do. You are a silly girl.

LINDA: What is your name, then?

BERYL: It's Father Gregory.

LINDA: *(She laughs.)* How can you be Father Gregory if you're my mother.

BERYL: You see, what I don't understand is how you can be so old if I am your mother.

LINDA: Because you're old.

BERYL: How old am I?

LINDA: How old do you think you are?

BERYL: Eighteen.

LINDA: Eighteen! In that case you had me before you were born.

BERYL: I don't understand what you mean, Linda. Anyway, I can't fall pregnant.

LINDA: Why not?

BERYL: Because I'm wearing this *(Pointing to the belt round her dressing gown.)*

LINDA: Is that going to protect you?

BERYL: Isn't it?

LINDA: Well, just as much as anything. I am as sure as I exist you're not going to get pregnant.

BERYL: That's good.

LINDA: *(Laughing.)* I'm surprised you even remember anything about that, mind you, not that you do.

BERYL: I remember, Linda.

LINDA: Do you, funny Mrs Queen. What do you remember?

BERYL: I remember being in bed with him.

LINDA: With whom?

BERYL: Well, there was that man

LINDA: Which man?

BERYL: *(Giggling.)* That man who lived with us.

LINDA: There were so many. Don't you remember mum, you used to have loads of lodgers.

BERYL: And there was one, he used to, ooohh, he was a one!

LINDA: What do you mean?

BERYL: He used to, ooh Linda. You're too young to hear about these things. You should speak to your mother about them.

LINDA: You are my mother.

BERYL: No I'm not, dear.

LINDA: Who was the man?

BERYL: Which man is that?

LINDA: The man you used to…

BERYL: Used to what, dear?

LINDA: The man you used to…. sleep with.

BERYL: Oh I always sleep by myself, dear.

LINDA: The man you used to make love to.

BERYL: Oh do you mean Joe?

LINDA: Joe!

BERYL: Ooh we used to laugh, trying to keep it all quiet from my daughter. I told him not to worry, she was far away, right at the bottom of the house. And I was right at the top. I had a daughter then, you know. But he didn't want her to know. Ever so thoughtful he was. Didn't want her to worry about these things. You know how girls might think their mum will be taken away from them. Have you had a little girl? Oh, then you'll know. You can understand what they're like, little girls. We used to dance. In my room, when everyone was asleep. We'd dance and dance. He was a lovely dancer. Ooh, he could dance, that one. I loved to dance. I still dance, look

(and she dances.)

You see. Can you dance, dear?

LINDA: What happened to him?

BERYL: I can dance. I often dance. I dance and I dance.

LINDA: What happened to Joe?

BERYL: Who's Joe?

LINDA: The man you were talking about.

BERYL: I was talking about my breakfast. I'm hungry Linda. I want my breakfast. I want eggs.

LINDA: What happened to Joe?

BERYL: Joe ho ho! I want my breakfast!

LINDA: I'm not going to give you anything until you tell me what happened to Joe.

BERYL: I don't know any Joe.

LINDA: You do. You were just talking about him.

BERYL: I was talking about my breakfast.

LINDA: You used to dance with him, laugh behind your daughter's back. My back. While I was asleep. You were laughing, dancing and laughing.

BERYL: I don't know what you're talking about, Linda. You're frightening me. You're making me scared. I just want my breakfast. I'm hungry!

LINDA: Tell me about Joe. What happened to Joe? What did you do to Joe?

BERYL: Nothing. I don't know any Joe.

LINDA: How could you have slept with Joe!

BERYL: I sleep alone. I always sleep alone. You can ask her. That woman, the one who lives here. She knows.

LINDA: You slept with him. With Joe. My Joe.

BERYL: Who are you? Where's that one who was here? What's your name?

LINDA: But he was mine!

BERYL: *(Shouting.)* Linda! Linda, come quickly. Where are you? Where are you?

LINDA: You wicked woman. What happened to him? What did you do to him?

BERYL: Help! Help me someone!

LINDA stares at her mother. BERYL backs into a corner.

BERYL: Linda! Linda, where are you?

LINDA: *(Softly.)* Oh my god. What did you do ….

BERYL is distressed and starts biting her buttons, and pulling at her hair.

LINDA watches her.

There is a knock at the door. BERYL rushes to open it. SAHID comes in.

BERYL: Linda! The post is here.

SAHID: I'm not the postman.

BERYL: Oh, aren't you, dear. I could have sworn you looked familiar.

SAHID: I am familiar. It is me, Sahid Khan.

BERYL: Oh dear, silly me. Who did you say, dear?

SAHID: Sahid…

BERYL: Linda. It's Sa, something. That's a funny name.

LINDA has stood up. She is embarrassed at seeing SAHID, not knowing how much he has seen.

LINDA: I'm sorry, I must, just, my face. I need to wash. Get dressed.

BERYL: But I want some cheese and biscuits.

LINDA: What?

BERYL: It's lunch time.

LINDA: Lunch time?

BERYL: I want cheese and biscuits.

LINDA: I'll go get it.

She exits.

SAHID sits down as does BERYL.

BERYL: Did you say you're from the war office?

SAHID: I'm a social worker. Your social worker actually.

BERYL: Does the war office do that these days?

SAHID: *(Pause.)* Yes.

BERYL: *(Shouting to LINDA.)* Did you know that Linda? The war office sends round soldiers.

SAHID: How are you feeling today, Beryl? Mrs Swallow.

BERYL: You can call me Beryl, dear. What did you say your name is. Officer...?

SAHID: Khan.

BERYL: Officer Khan.

SAHID: Sahid...

BERYL: Officer Sa, what, dear?

LINDA enters with the cheese and biscuits

BERYL: That looks good. Can I have some?

LINDA: It is for you.

BERYL: Oohh, thank you. *(To SAHID.)* She's my sister, you know. Come over from, where have you come from dear?

LINDA: The moon.

BERYL: Really? *(Laughing.)* No you haven't. You haven't, have you? The moon? No. She does like a laugh.

LINDA: Are you allowed to still be her social worker?

SAHID: Well strictly, I shouldn't. Not once I, you know, with the client. Or the client's daughter.

LINDA: Not the client, please!

SAHID: I have to keep it really quiet, but there's no one else to take on the case. I mean, professionally I really should ...

LINDA: But we're too much of a case, is that it? No-one was prepared to take us on?

SAHID: No, everyone's so busy. The case load, it's just crazy.

LINDA: Crazy caseload of crazy people.

SAHID: I'm trying to get some extra care. I mean, there's support you can have, more care. Memory retraining classes. They can start next week. Day care, just one day a week, initially. And then, the homes are good, you know. I mean, the manager at Beech Lodge is great, fantastic manner with the residents. *(Takes out brochures.)* I know there's no garden, but Oakwood is good too *(Passes a brochure.)* … The staff are great there. Really caring, not patronising. And because they're so close, you could go in every day, any time. You just go in, help with her. It's not a problem at all.

BERYL starts to laugh.

BERYL: I know what you're doing!

LINDA: Oh God!

SAHID: It's ok. Hello Beryl.

BERYL: Joe? Is that you, Joe?

LINDA: No mum. This isn't Joe.

BERYL: You leave my mother alone, you hear.

LINDA: It's me, mum. Linda.

SAHID: I'm Sahid, Beryl. Not Joe.

BERYL: Why does everyone lie to me. Tell me the truth. I can take it!

LINDA: Ok, you want the truth, it's Joe.

BERYL: Joe? *(Quite coquettish.)* Is that you, Joe?

LINDA: No, it bloody isn't! It's Sahid.

BERYL: Is it you Joe?

LINDA: Mum, have you finished your food?

SAHID: Tell me about Joe.

LINDA: Joe's in the past.

SAHID: Who is he?

LINDA: He's … not real.

SAHID: But he was

LINDA: Yes. He lived with me for many years. There *(Pointing to the bedroom.)*

51

SAHID: But

LINDA: and here *(Beating her head.)*, *(Beating her heart.)* and here.

BERYL: Linda. I'm finished. I ate it all up. Can I have an egg now. It's breakfast time and I want an egg.

LINDA: But not anymore.

BERYL: Is it Sunday today? I want to see Father Gregory.

No-one answers her.

BERYL: Shall we dance? I like to dance. We can put on a record on the record player. Something to dance to. Do you like to dance? I do. I always used to dance. Who did I use to dance with? It was a man. I remember him. We used to dance, when you were asleep.

LINDA: That was Joe.

BERYL: That's right. Joe. We used to dance.

SAHID: Joe? The same Joe?

LINDA: Yes.

SAHID: So he was real, Joe. Or is he just in your mother's head too? In her heart too?

LINDA: *(To BERYL.)* Sahid thinks Joe isn't real, mum.

BERYL: Joe. *(Laughing.)* Why would he think a thing like that? Oh, you are funny. Fancy that!

SAHID: Where is he?

BERYL: Where's Joe? He's upstairs. He's upstairs, isn't he Linda.

SAHID: There is no upstairs.

BERYL: Isn't there? There used to be.

SAHID: *(To LINDA.)* Was he, someone you loved when you were little? Was he, your father?

BERYL: Who? Joe? Oh no. Joe wasn't her father. No, that other man was her father. But he... who was your father, Linda?

LINDA: Not Joe.

BERYL: No, Joe was. Joe was my father.

LINDA: Joe was my mother's lodger. And it turns out, he was also my mother's lover.

BERYL: Ooh, Linda. Don't tell him *(She giggles, girlishly.)* What will he think of me!

LINDA: I'm sure he's heard worse, mum.

BERYL: He was very nice. He was very good with my daughter. He really looked after her well. Treated her like she was <u>his</u> daughter. Spent time with her, you know. And I'd wait for him to come to me, and we'd dance and dance. Can you dance? I love to dance. Put on a record, Linda. Let's dance. I want to dance. I want to dance! Nobody will dance with me! Who'll dance with me? Joe. Joe will. *(Calling as she exits.)* Joe! Joe!

BERYL exits. LINDA just watches her and doesn't move.

LINDA: I kept it a secret too, you see. It's embarrassing, telling your mother about, sex. I hated the thought of her knowing what I was doing. I knew she'd laugh at me, mock me. Stupid little girl, trying to be grown up. I was sixteen. I felt grown up. *(Pause.)* And then, I became pregnant, and there was no one else to turn to. So I told my mother.

SAHID: So what happened to Joe?

LINDA: Who else do you tell, if not your mother,

SAHID: And Joe? What happened to him?

LINDA: That's what girls do, don't they? They tell their mother. *(Beat.)* He hadn't been around for long. It's not as though he'd been there for months and months. Years and years. I didn't know about him and my mother. No wonder she... if I'd known I wouldn't've ...

SAHID: slept with him?

LINDA: ... told her.

SAHID: That you were pregnant.

LINDA: But I had to tell someone. Who could I tell?

SAHID: What about Joe?

LINDA: I never had a chance to tell Joe.

SAHID: Why?

LINDA: He'd gone.

SAHID: What do you mean?

LINDA: He didn't even, say goodbye.

SAHID: What?

LINDA: He just, didn't say goodbye. I don't know why he didn't say goodbye. Why do you think he didn't say goodbye?

SAHID: I don't know.

LINDA: I thought he loved me. That he'd be happy, about the baby.

(Pause.)

Everything my mother said was true. He just used me. He was always going to dump me. When he's had what I could give him, why would he stick around? What would he want with someone like you, someone fat and ugly, like you? You're too stupid and ugly to ever get yourself a real man. Someone who's not just going to use you. Use you and dump you.

SAHID: Your mother said that? And you believed it.

LINDA: Why wouldn't I?

SAHID: Because she shouldn't say things like that. Not a mother. And because it's not true. Because, you're beautiful.

LINDA stands looking at him and tears roll down her cheeks.

SAHID: You are beautiful.

SAHID goes to her and holds her tightly, kissing her face and stroking her. After a while, they sit together on the sofa. He is holding her.

You only realise what it is, when it happens. You think you know it, but only when it's real, do you really know it. It's funny, isn't it? I didn't ever think it would really happen to me.

LINDA: Why shouldn't it happen to you?

SAHID: Absolutely! Why the hell shouldn't it! *(Pause.)* I want to be here for you, Linda, be with you. I know how I feel with you. How you make me feel about myself. We're not teenagers where these feelings are so, unreliable. Why wait? What for? Why shouldn't we grab our chance now, while we have time, before we get

LINDA: Like her?

SAHID: Why should we wait?

LINDA: Why should we bloody wait!

SAHID: We can just, move in together. Now! Why wait?

LINDA: We could!

SAHID: We're our own bosses. Aren't we? We're not answerable to anyone. I swear I'll be good to you, Linda.

LINDA: And her?

SAHID: She's, getting so, she needs constant help. The brain, it just, gets worse and worse. These places, they provide specialist care. 24/7. That's what she needs. They're wonderful places these days.

LINDA: They do look after them, don't they?

SAHID: Yes.

LINDA: I mean, really well. Don't they?

SAHID: Really well. I mean, really, honestly. Talk to them, show pictures, you know, to stimulate, their memories. That's all they have, you know, long term

LINDA: Memories.

SAHID: Short term just

LINDA: Goes, doesn't it?

SAHID: Yeah. Just, long term, the rest, just goes.

LINDA: It's not as if, they get better. You don't get better. Do you?

SAHID: Just worse. Worse and worse. And then, nothing.

LINDA: And I'd be there. I'd go, every day. Wouldn't I? It's not as if, I'd abandon her. She wouldn't be abandoned. Would she?

SAHID: No.

LINDA: I'd go, meal times, things like that. They need to know, the people there, that she's not abandoned. That's it, isn't it?

SAHID: She'd never be abandoned.

LINDA: Of course not. She'd be, looked after. Well, she is looked after

SAHID: Professionally.

LINDA: I looked after her

SAHID: Of course, of course you did. I've never seen anyone look after, like you, really.

LINDA: I could do it, Sahid, I could, couldn't I?

SAHID: You deserve to be happy, Linda. It's your turn now.

Fade.

SCENE 3

BERYL is sitting on the sofa. She is staring in front of her and doesn't move or seem to notice anything. LINDA is watching her very anxiously.

LINDA: Mum, can you hear me now?

BERYL is vacant.

LINDA: Mum. Mum, Listen to me. Can you hear me? Can you? If you can, lift up your finger. Any finger. It doesn't matter. Just pick it up. Shall we try it? I'm going to ask if you want some tea. Now if you do, just lift your finger. Ok? Right, mum, do you want some tea?

No response at all.

LINDA: Does that mean you don't. Lift a finger if you don't. Do you want some tea? *(No response.)* Ok, let's try something else. Let's try egg. What about egg, nice eggy. Do you want egg? Your finger. Is there anything you want, just blink. You can blink, can't you?

SAHID barges in the door.

LINDA: Thank God you've come!

SAHID: I told you it would happen. Now will you believe me?

LINDA: What can we do?

SAHID: You've got to do what I've been telling you. You've got to sign these bloody papers.

BERYL: Everyone's always crying. That other girl's crying. Crying and performing.

LINDA: Mum, you're alright. Why didn't you speak? Do you want some egg?

BERYL: I don't know why she's crying. Crying and screaming? That other girl. The one downstairs. Huh? You. You over there. Go tell that girl to stop crying. Tell her they'll take her away. I can't stand her screaming like that.

SAHID: Who's crying? What, where?

BERYL: Just cries and cries. Downstairs. The girl. Listen to her. Can't you hear? Joe's gone.

SAHID: Joe?

BERYL: Joe? My Joe? Has he gone?

SAHID: Linda, what's she saying?

BERYL: He's gone because of her.

SAHID: Because of her?

BERYL: That stupid girl. It's all her fault. She took my Joe away from me. I want to dance and now he's gone.

SAHID: Why did he go?

BERYL: Good rubbish and good, bye. Good rid, rubbish. Good riddance. I want to dance. I want to dance.

BERYL goes to put on a record. She hasn't got the physical dexterity to do it and it is quite pathetic watching her try. After a short while LINDA goes to put it on. BERYL starts to dance very slowly and mournfully. LINDA goes back to SAHID and they watch intently.

Suddenly LINDA pushes SAHID towards BERYL… He moves hesitantly towards her.

BERYL: Joe! You've come to dance with me!

They dance.

BERYL: It's so good. It's been, ages, Joe. You didn't come last night. I was waiting for you. You don't want your Bewyl to wait for her Joe, do you? I get so lonely, waiting for Joe-Joe to come up to me. Why are you so quiet, Joe? Are you cwoss with your Bewyl?

It takes a while for SAHID to answer.

SAHID: No.

BERYL: Do you still love me?

SAHID: Yes.

BERYL: Oh goody goody goody.

She leans up to kiss SAHID but he resists. She struggles and is surprisingly strong and at the last moment he manages to move so that she kisses his cheek.

BERYL: You're a naughty boy tonight. You're playing hard to get! Shall we play that game where you're the little choir boy and I'm the vicar's wife, and then I'll come and find you and…

SAHID: No. Let's not. Not tonight.

BERYL: But I want to play. It's fun.

SAHID: What about, Linda?

BERYL: Who?

SAHID: Linda. Your daughter.

BERYL: What about her? She's alright. She's asleep. Shh.

SAHID: Is she alright?

BERYL: She's alright.

SAHID: She's crying.

BERYL: I know. She cries and cries.

SAHID: Why?

BERYL: Don't bother with her. Come, let's play. I can be the witch and you can be

SAHID: Why's Linda crying?

BERYL: The prince. You can be the prince.

SAHID: She's pregnant.

BERYL: The witch? Yes, the witch can be pregnant.

SAHID: I made her pregnant. Me, Joe.

BERYL: The witch?

SAHID: I made Linda pregnant.

BERYL: Joe? My Joe?

SAHID: Yes. It was me.

BERYL: My Joe, what?

SAHID: Yes, your Joe.

BERYL: Who are you?

SAHID: Joe.

BERYL: Joe? What are you saying? With Linda?

SAHID: …yes.

BERYL: But, you told me…

SAHID: I'm sorry.

BERYL: Sorry! You're sorry! You say you're sorry.

SAHID: *(No response.)*

BERYL: My Joe.

SAHID: No.

BERYL: Not Linda's Joe.

SAHID: Yes.

BERYL: Mine.

SAHID: No.

BERYL: Never Linda's.

SAHID: What about the baby?

BERYL: No baby.

SAHID: She's pregnant.

BERYL: No baby.

SAHID: I'm going to stay with Linda.

BERYL: No.

SAHID: Yes. I'm going to stay with her and the baby.

BERYL: No.

SAHID: Not with you.

BERYL: NOOO!

> *She is utterly distraught. She sobs and sobs and SAHID stands there watching her. LINDA is watching too. Nobody moves.*

BERYL: *(Becoming nasty.)* The police.

SAHID: What?

BERYL: I'm going to the police. I'm going to tell them. They'll take you in.

SAHID: Why would they do that?

BERYL: Because she's under-age! She's fifteen.

SAHID: No she's not.

BERYL: Yes she is.

SAHID: She told me she was sixteen.

BERYL: And I'm telling you she's fifteen. And if I say she's fifteen, the police will believe me. Because I'm her mother. So you'd better go. And if you don't get out of this house now, I'm going to call the police! And we'll see just how much you like being locked up in prison.

She suddenly snaps out.

Linda? Linda? I'm, I'm hungry Linda. I'm cold. I want to go to bed, Linda. I don't feel very well. I'm feeling very bad, Linda. I want to go to bed *(she dissolves into tears.)*

LINDA hesitates for a moment then goes to her and puts her arms around her.

LINDA: Shh. Don't worry. It's alright. Come, you can get into bed and I'll put your nice duvet on you and you can snuggle into bed and it'll be nice and cosy. Nice and cosy and you can have a little sleep.

BERYL: Yes.

LINDA: And when you wake up, I'll make you a nice cup of tea, and I'll be there, waiting. I'll always be there, waiting for you. For my Mrs Queen.

SAHID is isolated and sits looking at them, surrounded by his papers.

FADE TO BLACK

DUWAYNE

BASED ON THE BOOK 'STEVE AND ME'
BY DUWAYNE BROOKS

Characters

DUWAYNE
Aged 18 to 37

WHITE POLICEMAN
Various including Brian Paddick

BLACK POLICEMAN
Various

*White Policeman is designated (W)
in the script and Black Policeman (B)*

There are three or four actors: Duwayne, White Policeman, Black Policeman and Brian Paddick. If you feel it is appropriate, the White Policeman can play Brian Paddick, as he appears only in the final scene. The Policemen represent universal policemen, and in different scenes show different personalities, characteristics, or traits of policemen. In a sense it is like the facets of a diamond; each facet make up the whole, and such it is with these characters – the facets make up the Metropolitan Police as a whole.

Where one policeman ends one scene, the second policeman will start the next to create a flow to the whole play. Even though the scenes represent different times and periods, the movement, lighting, mannerisms and of course dialogue are such to enable the audience to understand these shifts.

It is a non realistic setting and the bare minimum of props is required. Boxes that may be used for different purposes such as a chair, bed, car, may be appropriate. Chairs are used for a car.

Video images may be used at certain points such as the Welling demonstration.

Duwayne was first performed 23 May 2014 at Devonshire Park Theatre, Eastbourne with the following cast:

Adrian DeCosta	DUWAYNE
David Ajao	POLICEMAN
Andy de Marquez	POLICEMAN
Paul Moriarty	BRIAN PADDICK

Director	Tony Milner
Production Manager	Paul Debreczeny

SCENE 1

Black.

Sound of a phone ringing.

Voiceover DUWAYNE on the phone

DUWAYNE: Ambulance. Quick. Please, quick... Well Hall road... he's dying. I don't think he's, it's all this blood, it's gushing, trickling now... my friend, he's, lying, on the ground, the blood,

DUWAYNE runs to where his friend is lying, dying.

We hear a police siren.

DUWAYNE: *(Crying.)* Why didn't you run?

The siren stops. POLICEMAN A walks over.

POLICEMAN A: *(W.)* What's happening?

DUWAYNE: We need an ambulance. Not police. Where's the fucking ambulance?

POLICEMAN A: No need for language.

DUWAYNE: He's bleeding. There's still a chance. *(Shouting.)* We need an ambulance. Can't you see!

POLICEMAN A: It's coming!

DUWAYNE: You gotta drive him to hospital. He's gotta get to hospital, quickly.

POLICEMAN A: No, we must wait for the ambulance.

DUWAYNE: But where is it?

POLICEMAN A: It's coming! They say it's coming!

DUWAYNE: He's gonna die. He needs the hospital.

POLICEMAN A: It'll be here. It's, just round the corner. You want to tell me what happened? Was there a fight?

DUWAYNE: No, can't talk now, already told officer, need ambulance. Where's the fucking ambulance? He's dying.

POLICEMAN A: It's coming

DUWAYNE: Can't you take him, look, the blood, it's frothing. He's still alive. What're you waiting for? Can't you stop the blood.

POLICEMAN A: It's coming, I'm telling you. Keep your shirt on. I need to ask you. How can I help if I don't know...

DUWAYNE: Stop the blood! Don't you know how to stop the blood! Isn't it your bloody job to know how to stop blood. Just simple fucking first aid. Don't you know! What fuck use are you? Stop the fucking blood.

POLICEMAN A: Look, I'm gonna have to use handcuffs on you, if you're not careful. You're getting hysterical.

DUWAYNE: You're all just standing around. Everyone's just standing around!

POLICEMAN A: It's, going all down the pavement.

DUWAYNE: He's losing so much blood.

POLICEMAN A: The ambulance is coming.

DUWAYNE: It's too late. The blood's stopped. It's, too late.

Siren of ambulance.

POLICEMAN A: Thank God.

DUWAYNE: The ambulance is here, it's here.

They move back away from him and watch.

DUWAYNE: Can I go with him. In the ambulance?

He registers no, moves back, watches them go – we hear the siren.

POLICEMAN A: Are you alright, mate?

DUWAYNE: Alright?

POLICEMAN A: What happened?

DUWAYNE: He's been

POLICEMAN A: Yeah. Who started it?

DUWAYNE: What?

POLICEMAN A: The fight? Who started it?

DUWAYNE: We were just …

POLICEMAN A: Yeah?

DUWAYNE: waiting for the bus.

POLICEMAN A: Who, you and, him?

DUWAYNE: Him. We were just waiting. They're around. Those boys, they're around. Down the road, that road. There. Go find them, they're just, now, go now!

POLICEMAN A: Did you get into a fight with them?

DUWAYNE: No! They attacked, they're still around. There were six, I think, they may be, six, I saw them, sort of, the one, he's got hair -that, like parts in the middle, you know. Like a curtain. *(Demonstrates parting.)*

POLICEMAN A: What? Calm down, mate. I don't know what you're on about.

DUWAYNE: They can't've gone far. They must be around. You gotta get them now. Go after them. Go now.

POLICEMAN A: Look, I got to talk to you. Get some answers. We've got to know.

DUWAYNE: They gonna get away.

POLICEMAN A: So, there was a fight, right?

DUWAYNE: They gonna get away.

POLICEMAN A: Look, you gotta help me. Now answer my questions.

DUWAYNE: We didn't know them. Just boys, white boys.

POLICEMAN A: They were white?

DUWAYNE: White, yes, white boys.

POLICEMAN A: You didn't know them? So who started the fight?

DUWAYNE: Fight? No fight. We were attacked.

POLICEMAN A: But nobody's gonna attack you for no reason. You must've started something.

DUWAYNE: They shouted 'what what nigger'. They kept shouting, 'what what nigger'. That's what they were shouting.

POLICEMAN A: Are you sure you didn't start anything?

DUWAYNE: Go find them. They were shouting 'what what nigger'.

POLICEMAN A: Ok. I heard you. Did you start it first?

DUWAYNE: We were waiting for a bus. The man said the 166 was on strike

POLICEMAN A: Which man?

DUWAYNE: I mean, that's why we went to the corner

POLICEMAN A: What corner?

DUWAYNE: To see if the 286 was coming. He had to get home you see. Or the 161. I gotta get to the hospital. Got to see

POLICEMAN A: You're not going anywhere at the moment. Now, who started the fight?

DUWAYNE: He might be dead.

POLICEMAN A: Nobody's dead.

DUWAYNE: How do you know? D'you know?

POLICEMAN A: Is he known to us?

DUWAYNE: He was going home.

POLICEMAN A: Look, I want to know who started the fight?

DUWAYNE: There wasn't a fight!

POLICEMAN A: So how come he got stabbed.

DUWAYNE: I don't know.

POLICEMAN A: But there must have been a fight.

DUWAYNE: I just thought he got hit.

POLICEMAN A: When did you think that?

DUWAYNE: When I saw

POLICEMAN A: You saw them hit him?

DUWAYNE: I saw them, hit him, with something
    (Shows downward thrust.)

POLICEMAN A: So who hit him then?

DUWAYNE: There were six. Five, or six. Yes, six.

POLICEMAN A: What did they look like?

DUWAYNE: One of them, the one, his hair was parted you know, like a curtain. He ran after me. Saw his hair

POLICEMAN A: So you were hit?

DUWAYNE: No, I ran. He didn't run.

POLICEMAN A: Who, the boy?

DUWAYNE: He didn't run. I don't know why.

POLICEMAN A: So was it here?

DUWAYNE: No. Down there. He ran.

POLICEMAN A: So he did run?

DUWAYNE: After he was attacked, then he ran.

POLICEMAN A: What's your name?

DUWAYNE: Duwayne Brooks.

POLICEMAN A: Duwayne. Is that, D u with two ns?

DUWAYNE: I must get to the hospital. His parents, they must, I must, somebody's got to

POLICEMAN A: Don't worry. They'll be told.

DUWAYNE: But nobody will know who he is.

POLICEMAN A: What's his name?

DUWAYNE: His name?

POLICEMAN A: Yeah!

DUWAYNE: Steve.

POLICEMAN A: Steve....?

DUWAYNE: Steve.

POLICEMAN A: Whatever!

SCENE 2

Light change. DUWAYNE goes and sits in a chair in the police station. He looks straight ahead. He is blank.

POLICEMAN B walks in.

POLICEMAN B: *(B.)* Duwayne? Duwayne Broooks?

    DUWAYNE doesn't answer.

POLICEMAN B: Is it true the boys shouted 'what what nigger?'

DUWAYNE: what what nigger.

POLICEMAN B: That's what they shouted?

    DUWAYNE doesn't answer.

POLICEMAN B: Are you sure they couldn't've said something else?

DUWAYNE still doesn't answer.

POLICEMAN B: They said 'what what nigger'? What what? Why what what?

You knew them, right? You'd met them before? Were you in, warring gangs? Is that it? Arranged to meet, and

DUWAYNE: We'd never seen them before.

POLICEMAN B: What were you doing in Eltham then? Why were you there, at that time? It doesn't make sense. Catching a bus? Why? Why there?

DUWAYNE doesn't answer. He is controlling himself to stop crying.

POLICEMAN B: This is ridiculous. How can we do anything if you don't answer.

Now, you telling me he said what what nigger. That what you saying?

To other policemen in the room.

Does that sound right, boys? You ever heard anything like that? What what nigger. What! Bloody outrageous! No provocation. Accept that?

Here, give us your trainers. We need to take a footprint.

DUWAYNE: What for?

POLICEMAN B: What for? You got something to hide?

DUWAYNE: You think I'm a burglar?

POLICEMAN B: Are you?

DUWAYNE: No!

POLICEMAN B: Well what were you doing out there then?

DUWAYNE: On our way home.

POLICEMAN B: Innocent people don't have nothing to hide. What you hiding?

DUWAYNE: Nothing.

POLICEMAN B: Nothing? You say they said what what nigger and you got nothing to hide?

There were gloves in his bag, the boy who died. Had he committed any burglaries recently?

DUWAYNE: What!

POLICEMAN B: Were you with him all night?

DUWAYNE: Yes!

POLICEMAN B: Did he leave your sight at all?

DUWAYNE: No!

POLICEMAN B: Did you go into a kebab shop?

DUWAYNE: No!

POLICEMAN B: And have an argument?

DUWAYNE: No!

POLICEMAN B: Because there was a half eaten kebab lying there.

DUWAYNE: We were on the bus. There's no kebab shop where we got off.

POLICEMAN B: A kebab shop owner phoned up about a fight between two black boys and white boys.

DUWAYNE: And we all look the same, do we?

POLICEMAN B: Don't be cheeky! Are you sure he didn't walk into the kebab shop?

DUWAYNE: He didn't walk into a kebab shop.

POLICEMAN B: Did you and him go to McDonalds. Harrass some white girls at McDonalds.

DUWAYNE: What! No. Nothing like that!

POLICEMAN B: Then their brothers came after you. Is that what happened?

DUWAYNE: No

POLICEMAN B: Are you sure?

DUWAYNE: Yes.

Fade slowly as POLICEMAN B asks

POLICEMAN B: Did you talk to anyone when you got off the bus at Eltham? Did anyone see you? Did your mother know where you were? Can she verify that? Did you…

As he's talking DUWAYNE slides off the chair and crawls over to his duvet, and wraps himself in it.

SCENE 3

Interspersed between knocking at the door and his phone ringing we hear.

VOICES: Duwayne! Duwayne! Are you alright?

> Duwayne. Are you ok?

> Open up! Duwayne. Open the door!

> *Still wrapped in the duvet DUWAYNE looks at the door, at the phone, both knocking, ringing, and doesn't move. It is then silent.*

DUWAYNE: You ask if I'm alright. You tell me what I need. You need this. You need that. I'm fine, I say. You need looking after. I'm fine.

> It's a terrible thing. You went through a terrible thing. What an awful, terrible thing, that's happened to Steve, to you. My God. Are you alright? Are you ok?

> I'm fine.

> What you gonna do? Where you gonna go?

> It's ok.

> You need a solicitor. You need someone, anyone, to protect, to look after, to see you're alright.

> No.

> What about your mum?

> I don't need my mum.

> Who do you need?

> I'm fine. It's ok.

> Who are these people? Do you know them?

> I don't know them.

> I've heard it's this gang from Eltham, white, racist buggers. Go round stabbing. You know that bloke, that guy who got stabbed last year, it's the same bloke, same lot, they go round stabbing us. They stab blacks. What what nigger? Yes.

> Everyone's telling me all sorts of names. These are the names. Have you heard of them? It's the Acourt brothers, Neil and Jamie, it's Norris, his father's like this *(fingers together.)* with the coppers. Gary Dobson, that's his name.

Luke Knight. And Norris, David Norris. Heard of them?
Well known. Everyone knows them. Everyone says it's
them. Know them?

What do they look like? Where do they hang out? Ahm,
not sure. Dunno.

What happened, Duwayne, they all ask. What happened
on the night? What did he do, what did you do? And then,
what happened, so why did, why didn't...

Why did you run? They ask.

Why didn't he run? They ask.

And I know that they're asking, did I do enough to save
my friend.

And I ask myself, did I do enough to save my friend.

Why can't you say who the people are? Don't you want
them to be caught? Can't you do a better sketch, they ask.

Are you ok, Duwayne. Are you ok?

You're not thinking about it, are you?

I'm fine. Just fine.

Are you ok, Duwayne? Have you recovered yet?

Ah no, you can't've recovered yet. No man. It hasn't hit
you yet. What you gonna do when it hits you? How you
gonna manage?

Did you hear, Duwayne, those boys, they're coming for
you! Everyone's saying it's you they're after now. You can
identify them, you can be a witness, so they're gonna get
you. They're gonna come and get you.

How safe are you?

How safe am I?

Those Norrises, they're bad'uns. Gangsters. Norris goes
around stabbing people. This is how he does it. Like this!

They're gonna come and get me. They're gonna come,
tonight, and get me. This chair, I'll put it right up against
the door. How can I get out, if I have to, fast. This window,

onto the ledge, along there, jump there, I could do that, jump, that's ok, and off. Yes, I can, it's ok.

If they come, I don't bloody care. They can come. Who gives a stuff? Do I care? Am I bothered? Fuck no. I don't give a shit. I don't

You've got to go to the Steve's house, they all tell me. You've got to tell them what happened. They deserve it.

I can't go there.

Why not? You got to go, man.

I can't.

They think I won't because they're cursing me. That she's calling me a ragamuffin, a thief, that they're saying it's all my fault.

I don't tell them it's because I won't be able to stop myself from crying.

I can't cry. I mustn't cry. I won't cry.

Yes? Steve? Did you call? Did you call me? I heard you say Duwayne. I heard you call me!

Steve, why didn't you run!

SCENE 4

POLICEMAN C walks over to DUWAYNE and pulls off his duvet and puts it on the side. DUWAYNE picks up the phone.

DUWAYNE: Imran? It's Duwayne. Look, are you gonna be able to get here? For the ID parade. ... I've never been to anything like this before. I'm sitting here, and I'm scared, Imran. I mean...... Well try, man. I mean, I don't even know how it works. Do they see me?... Are you sure? I don't want them to see me. They don't know what I look like. I want to keep it that way. If they can see me.... Well, if you're sure.... I can't see why you can't ... yeah sure but... Look Imran, this room is full of witnesses.... Why do you want me to do that?... Shouldn't you be getting their names...... You should be here Imran.

DUWAYNE: *(To POLICEMAN.)* Excuse me, Can I ask you something.

POLICEMAN C: *(W.)* Sure. Ask away.

DUWAYNE: What happened to the witness who was at the bus stop? Why isn't he here?

POLICEMAN C: Ahm...

DUWAYNE: I heard you leaked his name.

POLICEMAN C: No way!

DUWAYNE: Not on purpose.

POLICEMAN C: Never.

DUWAYNE: Now he won't come.

POLICEMAN C: I dunno who you been talking to, mate.

DUWAYNE: That's what I heard.

POLICEMAN C: Trust me.

DUWAYNE: How do I know my name won't be leaked?

POLICEMAN C: You can relax, Duwayne.

DUWAYNE: Like when I was brought here.

POLICEMAN C: We were with you.

DUWAYNE: In the minibus.

POLICEMAN C: We brought you.

DUWAYNE: And in the minibus, there's a white skinhead

POLICEMAN C: Lovely bloke, shame about the haircut.

DUWAYNE: And two other white guys.

POLICEMAN C: You got something against whites?

DUWAYNE: I'd just been in a white racist attack, right.

POLICEMAN C: Well

DUWAYNE: Who are these guys? Nobody introduced us. Nobody spoke. I was alone in a minibus with white skinheads. You think I shouldn't be scared? You think I should trust every young white boy I meet?

POLICEMAN C: But he was ok.

DUWAYNE: In that space, that confined space, anything could've happened.

POLICEMAN C: But it didn't, did it Dwayne.

DUWAYNE: No.

POLICEMAN C: So why do you worry so much.

DUWAYNE: Forget it.

POLICEMAN C: He'd been attacked. That boy, that skinhead.

DUWAYNE: I didn't know that at the time. Did I? I don't know who's guilty. Who's innocent.

POLICEMAN C: I'll be back in a minute.

POLICEMAN C goes away.

DUWAYNE gets up and goes to the window and looks out.

POLICEMAN C sees him and rushes over.

POLICEMAN C: Oi, get away from that window. You shouldn't be there. Hasn't anyone told you not to move? What did you see? Did you see people getting out of that van?

DUWAYNE: I wasn't paying attention.

POLICEMAN C: You didn't see people walk out of the police van?

DUWAYNE: *(Silence.)*

POLICEMAN C: Did you see them, I mean, see their faces.

DUWAYNE: No.

POLICEMAN C: Well just shut up about it.

POLICEMAN C: Ok Duwayne. Come. Before the ID starts, I just wanna take a sweet little picture of you.

DUWAYNE: What?

POLICEMAN C: Your picture. We need a picture. It's nothing.

DUWAYNE: What do you mean, it's nothing?

POLICEMAN C: I mean, it's nothing. Come on.

DUWAYNE: But, why?

POLICEMAN C: But why? Because we need a picture of you. A mug shot. Y'know.

DUWAYNE: No. I don't. I don't see why you need my picture. Look, I'm gonna have to check with my solicitor.

POLICEMAN C: What for, for Christ sake. It's just a picture.

DUWAYNE: But I'm not the guilty one here, am I? So why do you need my picture.

POLICEMAN C: Come with me.

DUWAYNE: No. I'll stand here. It's fine.

POLICEMAN C: Christ!

POLICEMAN B wheels on something to indicate a one way mirror (such as a coat rail.)

Right. Ok.

Ok, come on then. They're ready. Let's get the show on the road.

DUWAYNE walks up and down looking at the suspects (Audience). He is uncomfortable and anxious.

POLICEMAN C: Don't worry, Duwayne. They really can't see you.

Take your time. You can walk up and down, three, four times.

DUWAYNE: Ok.

He walks up and down once again.

POLICEMAN C: Anyone?

DUWAYNE: It's, ahm, *(He is unsure.)* that one.

POLICEMAN C: That's it.

DUWAYNE: I think so.

POLICEMAN C: Just think?

DUWAYNE: Yeah, no

POLICEMAN C: You gotta be sure.

DUWAYNE: Yeah, just that one.

DUWAYNE goes to sit down, anxious, not sure at all.

POLICEMAN C: D'you want a drink, Duwayne. Help yourself outa that fridge, yeah.

DUWAYNE: It's ok.

POLICEMAN C: You know, you coulda got them to turn, shout, make a stabbing motion, anything.

DUWAYNE: What?

POLICEMAN C: Yeah. Didn't anyone tell you? You can tell anyone in the line up to do anything you want.

DUWAYNE: Shall I...

POLICEMAN C: Too late now, mate.

POLICEMAN C: So, how do you think you did?

DUWAYNE: Ok.

POLICEMAN C: Ok. But we can't talk about the case.

DUWAYNE: That's ok.

POLICEMAN C: I can't even talk to you because I'm studying for exams. To get promotion.

DUWAYNE: That's ok.

Pause.

POLICEMAN C: Dunno why you picked out that bloke.

DUWAYNE: What?

POLICEMAN C: The one you picked out.

DUWAYNE: Why?

POLICEMAN C: Why d'you pick him?

DUWAYNE: Why do you think?

POLICEMAN C: It's cos people told you, people described them to you.

DUWAYNE: People are telling me things all the time.

POLICEMAN C: They told you what they look like, the Acourts.

DUWAYNE: They tell me lots of things. They tell me they got black hair. Then they tell me they got blond hair. They're six foot. They're three foot. I don't even listen anymore.

POLICEMAN C: You think you picked out the right one?

DUWAYNE: I think so.

POLICEMAN C: *(Softly.)* Wanker.

DUWAYNE: What?

POLICEMAN C: Nothing. You wait here.

POLICEMAN C leaves DUWAYNE sits. POLICEMAN D enters.

POLICEMAN D: *(B.)* There's serious allegations against you, Duwayne.

DUWAYNE: What?

POLICEMAN D: You gotta make a statement.

DUWAYNE: About what?

POLICEMAN D: About the ID parade.

DUWAYNE: But...

POLICEMAN D: Come sit here and make a statement.

DUWAYNE: I'm not making no statement without my solicitor being present.

POLICEMAN D: Well get him then.

DUWAYNE phones.

DUWAYNE: Hello, can I speak to Imran please. It's Duwayne Brooks... Can you tell him, it's very urgent please. ... I really must speak to him.... Can you ask him to get back to me please.

POLICEMAN D: Duwayne. You gonna be arrested if you don't give a statement. It's a very serious allegation. You can't have other people telling you who to pick out.

DUWAYNE: Nobody's told me who to pick out.

POLICEMAN D: You're in serious trouble, mate.

DUWAYNE: I'm doing my fucking best! I want to identify the right guys. What do you think? That I don't.

POLICEMAN D: I gotta tell you, Duwayne, that these allegations were made by a policeman.

DUWAYNE: Which policeman?

POLICEMAN D: The officer who was with you now. He advised his supervising officer that you asked him if you picked out the right boys.

DUWAYNE: I didn't!

POLICEMAN D: And, that you'd heard the killers were the Acourt brothers. And, that you picked out these boys because they matched the description given to you by your friends.

DUWAYNE: No that's crap.

POLICEMAN D: And because they looked like brothers. And that you were told by a mate of yours that you would recognise the Acourts because they've been to your school.

DUWAYNE: They haven't.

POLICEMAN D: And that you picked out one lad because he looked as if he'd just come out of a police cell.

DUWAYNE: No!

POLICEMAN D: Now I gotta tell you, Duwayne, these are very serious allegations.

DUWAYNE: But they're not true.

POLICEMAN D: I also heard that you're anti police.

DUWAYNE: What?

POLICEMAN D: You wanted to call the ambulance, not the police, when your friend was stabbed.

DUWAYNE: Yes.

POLICEMAN D: That you hadn't called the police because you wanted to exact your own revenge.

DUWAYNE: You, I, what!

POLICEMAN D: What do you have to say about that?

DUWAYNE: I can't fucking believe you.

POLICEMAN D: So you have nothing to say.

DUWAYNE: I have got something to say. It's this. Why has this officer, the one with the allegations, been assigned to my case?

POLICEMAN D: It's completely random.

DUWAYNE: And it's random, is it, just coincidence, that they say this officer, this is the one, isn't it, the one who worked on the Rolan Adams case. The Rolan Adams who was killed in a racist attack.

POLICEMAN D: So what? You seeing conspiracies now, Duwayne?

DUWAYNE: The one who was accused of trying to destroy the credibility of Rolan Adams' brother who was with him when he was attacked. Any similarities?

POLICEMAN D: I'd advise you to get your solicitor. Before you start getting into deep water.

DUWAYNE picks up the phone again.

DUWAYNE: Hello, Imran? You gotta help me, man. I gotta give a statement. ... Can't you.... Will that be alright? There is someone else here, a civilian. Yeah, I guess he's an 'appropriate adult'. Are you sure that's ok? I'd rather.... Ok, if you say so.

DUWAYNE sits opposite POLICEMAN D.

POLICEMAN D: Right. Let's begin. Now, you saying this officer made it all up?

DUWAYNE: Some of it's true. Most of it's lies.

POLICEMAN D: You can't say lies. Who they gonna believe? You or an office of the Met with ten years' experience.

You gotta say, he misunderstood you.

Maybe you didn't say you were coached by friends as to what the boys looked like. But you talked about it. Right?

DUWAYNE: Yeah.

POLICEMAN D: Yeah, exactly how else could you have been able to pick them out if you'd not seen their faces? Maybe if the officer misunderstood what you were saying, this is a better way of saying it, right?

DUWAYNE: I suppose so.

POLICEMAN D: So, after the ID parade, you described the boys you picked out and your mates told you they sounded very much like the Acourts.

DUWAYNE: But they didn't know what they looked like.

POLICEMAN D: But it makes sense, doesn't it?

DUWAYNE: What does it matter. Fuck. I'm tired. Put it in. You're not listening to anything I'm saying anyway. What do I care.

SCENE 5

Video of Welling – or simply background noise of a demonstration. Video background of the protests and police presence. DUWAYNE is standing in front of a police fence (the sort used to control crowds.) He has a stick in his hands and is banging the fence. Sounds of a crowd shouting.

POLICEMAN E (B.) and F (W.) is in riot gear. They confront DUWAYNE.

DUWAYNE: Get the BNP out! Why are you protecting the BNP? They got nowhere to hide. Why are you in their neighbourhood. Why are you protecting those white racist bastards, bastard coppers. You fuckers. Come and get us if you think you can.

DUWAYNE gets hit with a truncheon. He runs away kicking and throwing punches indiscriminately. POLICEMAN E and F are involved in hitting others. All three meet up and confront each other menacingly. POLICEMAN E and F lift their arms shouting. DUWAYNE backs off, until he is cornered. DUWAYNE ducks and runs off stage. POLICEMAN E and F carry on hitting others with their truncheon, as they move off stage.

Light spotlights DUWAYNE, alone.

I did it for you Steve.

SCENE 6

In DUWAYNE's flat.

Radio on – Nelson Mandela speaks

Their tragedy is our tragedy. I am deeply touched by the brutality of the murder – brutality that we are all used to in South Africa where black lives are cheap.

DUWAYNE turns off the radio

DUWAYNE: Why aren't I meeting him? Why just them?

If it had been me, would it be my mum who's the national treasure? Would she be the hero? She wouldn't call Steve a ragamuffin. Outcast. Ragamuffin! I'm no fucking ragamuffin. I'm studying, working. I always have. Lives in a hostel so has to be a bad 'un. I live in a hostel because

I want my independence. I look after myself. I'm fuckin, independent.

If I had been with Mandela, they'd all know me, know my face.

DUWAYNE is anxious, nervous. He listens at the door to any sound. He looks out the window, up and down the street to see if anyone is coming. He is a bag of nerves.

DUWAYNE:

He hears a noise.

What's that?

They're coming to get me. They not gonna bother paying me off, they just gonna silence me. Why pay good money when a bullet is so cheap, a knife even cheaper. What they gonna do?

Shh

No. It's, shh

Nothing.

Gonna get some food.

Gotta sleep first. Gonna sleep.

Shh

Sleep. Sleep.

Gets into bed and covers himself completely with duvet.

SCENE 7

We hear the voice of DUWAYNE's solicitor as he emerges from his duvet.

SOLICITOR'S VOICE: What's he doing in a cell. Can someone please explain to me what ... Duwayne Brooks is the surviving victim of a racist crime. And you've got him stuck in a police cell! Get him out of there! At once!

DUWAYNE: Is this how solicitors talk to the police? Are you allowed to shout them down? Do they always do what you tell them? Wowwe!

He's a victim, she said. A victim. First time anyone's said that.

You haven't signed anything, she said to me, first off. Right, no comment, that's all you say. Right? Yes ma'am!

Enter POLICEMAN G. He sits opposite DUWAYNE.

POLICEMAN G: *(W.)* Don't you think it would be a good idea to cooperate for your own sake?

DUWAYNE: No comment.

POLICEMAN G: You do know you're being charged with rioting?

DUWAYNE: No comment.

POLICEMAN G: That this is a serious allegation and you could be sentenced to prison.

DUWAYNE: No comment.

POLICEMAN G: Off the record, Duwayne, your solicitor is causing no end of trouble. We just need to search your house. If you're innocent, what's the problem?

DUWAYNE: No comment.

POLICEMAN G: Look we know you live in the hostel, but your official address is your mum's. So now we gotta search your mum's house. Don't you want to spare her the hassle? You know we're gonna search it anyway. Find that identifying hat from Welling…

DUWAYNE: No comment.

POLICEMAN G: Oh piss off. Come on, let's go. And no, she's not coming in the car with you.

They get into the car. DUWAYNE is in the back seat.

POLICEMAN G: Lovely day, init?

That solicitor of yours, Jane, is it? I dunno who she thinks she is, coming into the station and bossing people about. She's only a bloody solicitor. I know what her problem is. She hasn't had it for ages. Dumb cow. That's her problem. She needs someone to give her one. That should calm her down a bit.

We know it was you, Dwaynne. Whatever you or your solicitor want to say. We know it was you and we're gonna get you. What's so special about you? Who do you think you are?

If I was you, I'd get that smirk off your face, if you know what's good for you.

The car stops and they get out. DUWAYNE is handcuffed.

POLICEMAN G: Right let's go through this bloody charade.

DUWAYNE and POLICEMAN G go into the house. POLICEMAN G looks around.

DUWAYNE: I gotta go to the toilet.

POLICEMAN G goes to check there are no windows there.

DUWAYNE: Aren't you gonna take the handcuffs off?

POLICEMAN G: You might try to escape.

DUWAYNE: He's already checked there's no way.

POLICEMAN G: Go!

DUWAYNE is in the toilet.

Look at me, Steve. In my mum's toilet with handcuffs on. What would you have said? You'd have laughed, I can see you. Pointing at me, How you gonna piss, you'd say. I'm gonna sit. That's what I'm gonna do!

SCENE 8

Video of suspects walking into court for the committal (not essential).

DUWAYNE is in court. POLICEMAN H has a radio earpiece on.

POLICEMAN H: *(B.)* This way Mr Brooks. Just keep straight on.

DUWAYNE: *(Frightened.)* Can my friend come with me?

POLICEMAN H: He can't come into the court. He can wait here.

DUWAYNE: But I need someone I can trust.

POLICEMAN H: We're the police, Mr Brooks. You can trust us.

DUWAYNE: Yeah, like sending a witness statement to the suspects with my address on it.

POLICEMAN H: Don't worry, Mr Brooks.

DUWAYNE: Don't worry? I mustn't worry that the suspects know where I live.

POLICEMAN H: Look at all the police here. It's to ensure your safety. No-one can get at you, Mr Brooks. Trust me. Come sit here in this waiting room.

DUWAYNE: Who are those people there?

POLICEMAN H: Witnesses.

DUWAYNE: Who's that woman?

POLICEMAN H: That's Mrs Knight, there.

DUWAYNE: Luke Knight's mum? The suspect?

POLICEMAN H: Nothing to worry about. You ok, Duwayne?

DUWAYNE: Yeah. *(He is starting to panic.)*

POLICEMAN H: You want some water. You look, you're not gonna faint, are ya?

DUWAYNE: Yeah, water.

VOICE: DUWAYNE BROOKS

(DUWAYNE gets up and walks into the court. He stands straight. Spotlight on DUWAYNE. The italics show he is talking to the Judge. Otherwise it is an internal thought process. All else black...)

DUWAYNE: That's him! There. The one there. Look at him. I can see him. He's the one. I remember, I can see him now. They were walking there across the road. What, what's he saying? *Yes, the attackers, he's the one. He's the one that did it.* What? Was that what I said before. Is it the same? I needed time to prepare. I haven't had time to prepare. What am I supposed to say? What do they want? It's been two years since I made that statement. Am I saying the same thing? I gotta say the same. The stabber? *Yes, him. That one there. That is the one that I saw.* He was blond, blue eyes, he looked like him, no shit, it's not him. I can't remember. I didn't say that last time. Curtains, I said it was curtains. This one isn't curtains. Blonde, blue eyes, this one. No, it wasn't this one. No take it back, that's not what I mean. I meant the other one. Can't take it back. *Did I see their faces? Yes, I saw their faces.*

I saw their faces. But I didn't look at their faces. I didn't have time to look at all their faces. Don't they understand. I was in fear of my life.

Fleeting glance. *It was a fleeting glance. Just a fleeting glance.* Of course it was a fleeting glance. I never said anything else.

Steve screamed. (Shock sound from DUWAYNE). Nobody knew Steve screamed.

What's that? Steve's dad's crying. I gotta get out of here! Let me out!

I can go. I can leave. I'm going. Don't look, don't look at any of them. Go, just go, go, go.

SCENE 9

DUWAYNE is in his room. There is wild music on and he is dancing wildly, hysterically.

SCENE 10

DUWAYNE is sitting with POLICEMAN J (FRED). They are at The Old Bailey. DUWAYNE is nervous and anxious. It is the time of the private prosecution.

POLICEMAN J: *(W.)* Have you been to the Old Bailey before, Duwayne?

DUWAYNE: No.

POLICEMAN J: Court 1? It's where all the major murder trials take place.

DUWAYNE: Is that supposed to make me feel important?

I wanted a screen. But they wouldn't do it. They did it for other witnesses. They all gonna know who I am now.

POLICEMAN J: Try relax. There isn't any evidence, you know. They're desperate, if you ask me. There's no forensics, no camera shots, no real eyewitnesses. They're all depending on you, Duwayne. The stakes are so damn high. If they go free they won't be able to be tried again, because of double jeopardy.

DUWAYNE: My auntie says it's a trap. They're gonna use me, break me down and then blame me. What do you think, Fred? It's a trap, innit?

POLICEMAN J: Your solicitor

DUWAYNE: She didn't have the power to stop the case.

POLICEMAN J: And would you have wanted, not to give evidence? The only witness refuses to give evidence.

DUWAYNE: What the hell can I do! My psychiatrist has written a report saying I'm suffering from post traumatic stress disorder, that I'm unfit to give evidence. They've got the report but they still go ahead with the private prosecution. They know I'm unfit, but they're not interested. They talk to the press as if they know they gonna get a conviction because they've got me. Me! The star fucking witness! Which way can I turn? If I walk away, I'll be the scapegoat. If I mess up the evidence, I'll be the scapegoat. Where can I go? Nobody will ever speak to me. And when are the rumours gonna start, he was paid, bought off. Chickened out.

POLICEMAN J: Just stick to what you know, Duwayne. It'll be alright.

DUWAYNE: But I don't stand a chance. Doesn't anybody care?

DUWAYNE is terribly upset.

Pause.

POLICEMAN J: *(W.)* I had a friend, a copper, who worked in immigration. He told me this story of a man who went to Jamaica to import crack cocaine. Anyway, he was followed by British Intelligence, right. So this man went to an obeah man, you know, black magic, white magic, protection, whatever. So the magic man casts a spell so that when the drug dealer gets stopped at the airport, security would see coffee and not cocaine. Now, they knew he'd been buying cocaine. They'd seen it, spies, and when he got to Heathrow they were waiting for him. But, when they opened the bag, searched the bag, methodical like, what did they see but coffee. They searched and searched but could only see coffee. So they let him go. But they were so sure about this bloke so that when he got outside to get a taxi, another set of immigration officers searched his bag and found cocaine. No coffee. Cocaine.

DUWAYNE: What happened?

POLICEMAN J: He got off. Because he claimed it had been planted. Because the first lot didn't find it.

DUWAYNE: But in my case, they didn't find the evidence not because of black magic, but because of incompetence, corruption.

POLICEMAN J: Anyway, good to see you talking again, mate.

POLICEMAN J is caught by his earpiece.

POLICEMAN J: Right. Ok. Yes. Will do.

Duwayne. It's all over. The judge has come back. They say your evidence is inadmissible. It's been discredited. It's difficult to convict on fleeting glance evidence. They've got away with it.

DUWAYNE: But I always said it was a fleeting glance.

POLICEMAN J: Yeah.

DUWAYNE: There was no other evidence.

POLICEMAN J: No. Only yours.

DUWAYNE: It's all over.

POLICEMAN J: Yes.

DUWAYNE: So, that's it. I'm the one they blame.

POLICEMAN J doesn't respond.

DUWAYNE: They not gonna say they never had a case. They just gonna say, he lost it for us. Main witness changed evidence. Nothing about that they never gave me my statement to read.

POLICEMAN J: That is outrageous.

DUWAYNE: Three years later, how do they expect me to

POLICEMAN J: Everybody's always given their statement before they get into court.

DUWAYNE: Twenty minutes they gave for me to look at it. Quickly, the judge said. Go read it. You got twenty minutes to read it. Fuck, I couldn't even focus on the words.

POLICEMAN J: Outrageous.

DUWAYNE: What are they all gonna say? You lost it for your friend.

POLICEMAN J: They won't understand.

DUWAYNE: That's Duwayne Brooks. That's the one that was with him when he died. He ran, left his friend, then went and changed his story. Don't you feel bad, letting them guys get away? How could you have let them go to court and you knew you were going to change your story? You must have been paid off.

I can't see it properly, you know. Even now, my head won't let me see exactly what happened. Everything that happened, that night.

Goes into his duvet.

SCENE 11

Light change, flickering in front of him (Indicating TV). DUWAYNE unfurls from his duvet as we hear:

VOICE FROM TV: He was a primary victim of the racist attack. … also the victim of all that has followed, including the conduct of the case and the treatment of himself as a witness and not as a victim.

Mr Brooks was stereotyped as a young black man … We believe that Mr Brooks' colour and such stereotyping played their part in the collective failure of those involved to treat him properly and according to his needs.

In her written statement made at the scene PC Bethel described Mr Brooks as *"very distressed"* and *"very excitable and upset"*. In her answer to a 1994 questionnaire she said that he was *"aggressive, anti-police, distressed and unhelpful"*. To the Kent police she said that Mr Brooks was *"powerful and physically intimidating"*, and that his behaviour was *"horrendous"*. … the evidence does show how racist stereotyping can develop. We do not believe that a young white man in a similar position would have been dealt with in the same way.

There were fundamental errors. The investigation was marred by a combination of professional incompetence, institutional racism and a failure of leadership by senior officers.

DUWAYNE: Bloody fucking hell!

Enter POLICEMAN K.

POLICEMAN K: *(B.)* Hello Mr Brooks. I'm from the Black Police Federation. We met

DUWAYNE: We did?

POLICEMAN K: I said you should talk to me if you had any problems.

DUWAYNE: There is one thing

POLICEMAN K: Yes?

DUWAYNE: It intrigues me.

POLICEMAN K: What is it?

DUWAYNE: They're tapping my phone.

POLICEMAN K: What makes you believe that?

DUWAYNE: Well, I haven't paid my bills for twelve months. And my phone is still working.

POLICEMAN K: That doesn't mean it's being tapped.

DUWAYNE: No?

POLICEMAN K: It could just be an oversight.

DUWAYNE: Do you know anyone else who hasn't paid their bill for twelve months and their phone is still working?

POLICEMAN K: We gotta do our job, Mr Brooks.

DUWAYNE: So you gotta, stop and search, stop me in my car and search for drugs, check out who the car really belongs to. They've had me so often for taking and driving away that the officer at Lewisham sees me and says straight out – is it a White Fiat Uno? Ok, that's his. Let him go!

POLICEMAN K: If we don't do stop and search, crime rates will soar, Mr Brooks.

DUWAYNE: Come on mate, we're both black. Tell me what's really going on here.

POLICEMAN K: It's destroying morale, that's what it's doing. People don't like to be called racist, if they're not. Some of my friends are breaking down. Crying. Grown men crying. They don't like the label.

DUWAYNE: My heart bleeds for them.

POLICEMAN K: You don't like being called a mugger, if you're not.

DUWAYNE: I've never mugged anyone in my life. That doesn't stop white women grabbing their handbags as I walk down the street. Too many young black men have been arrested for no reason and then let free. It's been six years! Tell me what's changed!

POLICEMAN K: The Met has changed. Police have changed. Things are different, Mr Brooks. You'll see.

SCENE 12

Knock on the door. DUWAYNE opens and lets POLICEMAN L enter.

POLICEMAN L: *(W.)* Morning sir.

DUWAYNE: Thank you for coming.

POLICEMAN L: You said it's an emergency.

DUWAYNE: It is. My car's been broken into.

POLICEMAN L: And you think that's an emergency.

DUWAYNE: Yes.

POLICEMAN L: Cars are broken into every day of the year, sir. If everyone thought

DUWAYNE: I'm not everyone. I'm a target.

POLICEMAN L: No, Mr Brooks, you're not. But, well, perhaps you'll tell me why this is an emergency.

DUWAYNE: It's an emergency because I've been targeted.

POLICEMAN L: Why would you be targeted, Mr Brooks.

DUWAYNE: Because I was on the march to Downing Street yesterday. And people high up in the Met didn't like it.

POLICEMAN L: Well, we'll put up a board asking for witnesses.

DUWAYNE: And that's the best you can do?

POLICEMAN L: We haven't got the manpower to go door to door for your tool box and deodorant, Mr Brooks.

DUWAYNE: Listen here. I'm getting sick of it. It's happening all the time. I say I'm gonna sue the police for racial harassment and suddenly things start happening to me. My car gets broken into. Six, eight times. Never before. And extraordinary coincidence that it happens even when I sleep at different places, quiet roads where nothing ever seems to go wrong. Amazing, people say, we never have any trouble on our road. Is it just me or is there some sort of funny correlation, shall we say, between me talking publicly about Macpherson's findings, my experience with you guys, and things happening to my car. All the time.

POLICEMAN L: There's very little we can do.

DUWAYNE: You're as good as your word.

SCENE 13

Enter POLICEMAN M.

POLICEMAN M: *(B.)* Hello Duwayne. I've now been assigned to you, to look after all your needs and provide duty of care.

DUWAYNE: Oh yeah. You know as well as me, the only reason they've put you here is because you're black.

POLICEMAN M: If I thought that, Duwayne, I wouldn't have taken the job.

DUWAYNE: Bullshit. Go look after the black boy, you're black, it looks good. We're showing we care. But why you interested? Just so that you can say, yeah I dealt with Duwayne Brooks. I was part of it, the Stephen Lawrence story, the biggest upheaval the Met has faced.

POLICEMAN M: I'm just doing my job. It's no ego trip, believe me.

DUWAYNE: What are you doing about the police harassing me?

POLICEMAN M: I don't believe it is the police. The police have no business doing things like that.

DUWAYNE: I know they have no business doing it. It doesn't mean they aren't though, does it? Why aren't the officers making house to house inquiries?

POLICEMAN M: Somebody would have told us by now, if they'd seen anything.

DUWAYNE: But your job is to do that. Why am I just getting bullshit all the time. Duty of care. Looking after your needs. Go round, house to house. That'll meet my needs.

POLICEMAN M: Have you got proof that things were stolen? Was the stuff marked? Did you park in a safe place where there were lights?

DUWAYNE: Does everybody have to have their stuff marked? Why just me? Does everybody have to park where there are lights? Why just me? You all talk of respect, ooh, come and look at our new Racial and Violent Crimes Taskforce headquarters, Mr Brooks. Come, look how important you are, look how we value you, Mr Brooks. What changes do you recommend, Mr Brooks. Look at our racial awareness training, Mr Brooks. We'd like to consult you on it, Mr Brooks. The only consulting I want is for them to put surveillance on my car. Why don't they?

SCENE 14

DUWAYNE is in his car.

DUWAYNE: *(Shouting behind him.)* Stupid wanker *(shows the sign.)*

We hear a siren and POLICEMAN N and O march up to him aggressively

POLICEMAN N: *(W.)* You said stupid wanker. Get the fuck out of your car.

POLICEMAN N tries to grab the keys and DUWAYNE doesn't let him. Between the two policemen they pull him out of the car, punch him, put handcuffs on, elbow him in the face and push him to the FLOOR

POLICEMAN N: *(B.)* Get on the floor, you fucking nigger.

He beats him some more.

POLICEMAN O: You stupid wanker. Who the fuck do you think you are? Where are your bruises? Hey, hey, where are your bruises? I can't see them. Haven't you got any bruises?

He takes out from DUWAYNE's car a metal rod, a Stanley knife, and a cheque book.

POLICEMAN N: Aggressive weapons, stolen car, stolen money. You're nicked, you bastard.

POLICEMAN N kicks him.

SCENE 15

DUWAYNE is in a police station. POLICEMAN N is the custody officer at the station. POLICEMAN O is the arresting officer.

DUWAYNE: Why have I been put in a cell for an hour?

POLICEMAN N: *(W.)* Your detention is authorised because you have offensive weapons in the car.

DUWAYNE: The arresting officer didn't follow any of the correct procedures. Did you?

I want to see the search record.

(POLICEMAN N gives it to him.)

Have you seen what it says here? Look at the reasons for stopping me. On approaching the car I noticed an offensive weapon. How could he see it from his car? And the offensive weapon? I'm a photocopier technician. They're tools for my work!

POLICEMAN N: *(Taking up a piece of paper.)* Ok, Mr Brooks, we can see that it is your car, and that the weapons were in fact tools. You can go now.

DUWAYNE: Have you read what he's written?

POLICEMAN N: Can you leave the station now please. We're very busy.

DUWAYNE: Just like that. What about an apology?

POLICEMAN O takes him by the collar and throws him out the station.

SCENE 16

POLICEMAN P is holding DUWAYNE and pushes him into a seat.

POLICEMAN P: *(B.)* Sit here please.

POLICEMAN Q: *(W.)* A serious allegation has been made against you of attempted rape. You have been arrested for the attempted rape and indecent assault of Miss Judy Smith.

We need to search your room, Mr Brooks. Can you tell me which is your room in the hostel.

DUWAYNE: You can't search it without me being there.

POLICEMAN Q: Oh yes we can, Mr Brooks.

DUWAYNE: Ok, go on then, search it.

POLICEMAN Q: Well we don't know which room is yours.

DUWAYNE: If I'd tried to rape someone in my room, she'll know where my room is and she can tell you.

POLICEMAN Q: Ok Mr Brooks, we're going to put non-cooperation on your file.

Listen Mr, Brooks. I'm trying to help you. But I can only help you if you help yourself. You've got to give us something to go on. Something I can give to my sergeant. I don't want you to be here all night. I want you to be able to go home. Have a think about it.

DUWAYNE: What's there to think? It's a bit odd, isn't it? All these video cameras and all sorts, but you don't have any evidence. You don't even have enough evidence to concoct a story.

POLICEMAN Q: Wipe that smile off your face, Mr Brooks. This is a serious charge against you. If I was you, I'd take these proceedings very seriously indeed. In fact, you're not getting bail.

DUWAYNE: I see exactly what's happening. You think it'll be good, convicted sex offender takes on the police. Who would you trust? But there's no way you gonna win this mate, because it's all lies.

POLICEMAN Q: Let's see how you feel after a little spell in the cells, shall we?

DUWAYNE stands in a cell. It is disgusting. The smell from the toilet is revolting. He sits down. He is freezing cold.

DUWAYNE: *(Calling.)* Hello.

POLICEMAN R: *(B.)* What?

DUWAYNE: I'm freezing. I need a cover.

POLICEMAN R: No covers available.

DUWAYNE: What about a pillow.

POLICEMAN R: No pillows available.

DUWAYNE: I suppose no hot water is available for a drink is it?

POLICEMAN R: You can have tea.

DUWAYNE: I just want hot water.

POLICEMAN R: You can have sugar.

DUWAYNE: Look, I'm expecting my jacket from my friend. Do you know if it's come yet?

POLICEMAN R: Not allowed.

DUWAYNE: What do you mean, not allowed?

POLICEMAN R: Might have something in it.

DUWAYNE: Why don't you just check the pockets?

POLICEMAN R: Not allowed. Might be something in there. Seen the newspapers?

DUWAYNE: Funny that. They wouldn't let me just pop out.

POLICEMAN R: Don't be cheeky. Lawrence Friend on Attempted Rape Charge. Evening Standard.

DUWAYNE: I wonder who told them. They must have been told five minutes after the charge.

POLICEMAN R: Can't imagine.

DUWAYNE: Course not.

POLICEMAN R: You're here for the weekend, mate. Enjoy yourself.

SCENE 17

DUWAYNE is in court. POLICEMAN K (FRED.) comes up

POLICEMAN K: *(W.)* Hello there Duwayne.

DUWAYNE: Ahh, hello Fred. You on duty at court today?

POLICEMAN K: Yeah. I manoeuvred it a bit. Wanted to see how you was getting on.

DUWAYNE: I'm fine.

POLICEMAN K: What you been doing?

DUWAYNE: I had to stay in Birmingham for two months. Bail conditions. Not allowed back into London, in case I harass 'the victim'.

POLICEMAN K: Bail?

DUWAYNE: £20,000! On a Friday evening too.

POLICEMAN K: What?

DUWAYNE: They thought I wouldn't be able to make the bail. But there's good people around.

POLICEMAN K: The charge has been downgraded to indecent assault.

DUWAYNE: They clutching at straws. There's no evidence because nothing happened but that's not stopping the CPS pursuing it.

POLICEMAN K: Why they doing it?

DUWAYNE: To get at me. Discredit me. It's nothing to do with anything or anyone other than me. Imagine the negative publicity if they pulled out now. 'Duwayne Brooks, the man racially stereotyped by the police, has all charges against him dropped'. It's not gonna do the Met's reputation any good, is it?

POLICEMAN K: I don't understand what's going on, Duwayne.

DUWAYNE: Fred, listen to me. That girl, the 'victim', she came to my room. I didn't invite her, I didn't want her. My girlfriend phoned and I told the girl I was going. She wanted a lift home and I said no, and went. She got pissed off. After I left, she rang the police and said she'd been assaulted and could they come and get her. When the police came she changed her story and said nothing had happened but could they give her a lift home anyway. But the police wanted a charge so they encouraged her, pushed her. Gave her money.

POLICEMAN K: It smacks of desperation to get a conviction, mate.

DUWAYNNE: They got this mediator to look after her. The mediator goes to the police, and says, look, there's a real problem here, I've got grave doubts about the case. The girl said he didn't do anything, just sat there.

One day I swear this will come out, that they're setting me up. They're just, setting me up.

SCENE 18

DUWAYNE is sitting in a meeting with an officer from the Police Complaints Authority.

POLICEMAN S: *(B.) (He is anxious and doesn't make eye contact with DUWAYNE.)* As you know, we have put your complaint in the hands of the Kent constabulary. It is a serious complaint and we are taking it seriously, both of these complaints, against Officer Jones who refused to accept your complaint, and the behaviour to you concerning ten officers when, you know, on the night, after Stephen…

As you can see, Duwayne, the number of tasks we have to complete means it will take much longer than the normal 120 days. In fact, it could take six or seven months. But throughout we will be working at full capacity to resolve the complaint because we know, Duwayne, what happened to you and we wouldn't like it to happen to any members of our family or our friends.

In fact, Duwayne, we don't normally have big meetings with complainants, but because this is a special case, things are going to work differently.

Now, our problems are really finding time to interview each and every officer, them being available for us, and not giving us the runaround. It's going to be hard,

Duwayne. Officers go on sick leave sometimes, they take holidays, and we have to wait for them. We can give them appointments but ultimately we need to wait for them to make themselves available.

DUWAYNE: What about those who are about to retire?

POLICEMAN S: Well we are going to try our best to interview each and every officer as quickly as we can.

DUWAYNE: So are you going to interview the officers who are coming up for retirement first?

POLICEMAN S: Well, we don't have a schedule for interviewing yet.

DUWAYNE: So what you're saying is you don't know who you're going to interview, and you don't really believe you will interview any of them because the officers will just make themselves unavailable, especially those who are due to retire.

POLICEMAN S: Duwayne, you can rely on me. Nothing can stop the investigation.

DUWAYNNE: You telling me you're going to interview officers who are just about to complete their thirty years and walk off with their pensions?

POLICEMAN S: Those officers will have to speak. Though, of course, after the Kent police finish the investigation, the PCA can only recommend that officers be disciplined. Ultimately it is up to the Met, the Commissioner.

Anyway, it was good to meet you Duwayne. You do know, don't you, that Mayor Livingstone has ordered an inquiry into why you've been stopped so much.

Keep up the fight.

SCENE 19

DUWAYNE enters the spotlight, giving a speech.

DUWAYNE: They said it would be more than 120 days. What they didn't say was that it would take 900 days. For what! Officer Jones retired, as we knew he would. Of the ten officers we complained about, two were given a slap on the wrist, a written warning. Of the others, the PCA said that during their interviews, the officers had refused to cooperate. The PCA found that none of the officers who had refused to answer questions in interviews could be found to be racist or to have racially stereotyped me. And why? Because they had not told their side of the story.

It's as if the Macpherson inquiry has never happened. This is not acceptable. We can't accept it. But people don't know. They don't understand what is really happening in this country. They don't understand what is going on with the police and black people in this country. But one day they will. I can tell you, they will.

BRIAN PADDICK comes up from the audience.

BRIAN: Duwayne! Congratulations. That needed saying.

DUWAYNE: Mr Paddick. Thank you.

BRIAN: I was impressed.

DUWAYNE: Yes?

BRIAN: And pleased. It takes guts to stand up and tell the truth. I know who you are, you know.

DUWAYNE: Is there a picture in the Met of me, a wanted poster. If you see this geezer, stop him and search. Make his life a bloody misery.

BRIAN: *(Laughs.)* Yeah! I'm sorry for that. You know we're not all like that.

DUWAYNE: Really? You the good copper? Borough Commander of Lambeth. The one good copper in the Met?

BRIAN: Yeah! That's me! But there are more like me.

DUWAYNE: Easy to talk, isn't it?

BRIAN: Not only talk with me. I get rid of racist cops when I see them. Problem is they often get given their jobs back. But not by me.

DUWAYNE: So what happens to the one good apple in the barrel?

BRIAN: He develops a tough skin.

DUWAYNE: Is that enough to stop the rot?

BRIAN: You develop layers and layers.

DUWAYNE: Do you need them?

BRIAN: I know victimisation, Duwayne. I'm gay, openly gay, the only openly gay senior officer in the Met. Hadn't you heard?

DUWAYNE: Yeah.

BRIAN: I haven't been through what you've been through, though.

There's a lot of people think very highly of you, you know, Duwayne. Even some in the Met.

DUWAYNE: Thanks.

BRIAN: So what you doing, Duwayne. How's life treating you?

DUWAYNE: Well, when I'm not being stopped and searched, arrested, beaten up by you guys, life's good. I'm the best photocopier engineer in London.

BRIAN: *(Laughs.)*

DUWAYNE: Yeah. It's ok. Life goes on.

BRIAN: What you doing for your community?

DUWAYNE: Why do you think I should do anything?

BRIAN: Because I know what you are. What you're like.

DUWAYNE: And what's that?

BRIAN: Someone who doesn't take the easy road.

DUWAYNE: *(Laughs.)* To tell you the truth, I've registered a charity, a foundation. The Brooks Foundation for Victims of Crime.

BRIAN: Sounds good.

DUWAYNE: Yeah. But I haven't got round to the funding application yet.

BRIAN: Why not?

DUWAYNE: I need help. I went to the Tories. They put the phone down. Labour told me to fuck off.

BRIAN: And the Lib Dems?

DUWAYNE: I haven't been there yet.

BRIAN: Well you have now. And we're gonna help you.

DUWAYNE: Yeah?

BRIAN: Too bloody right! Listen Duwayne. There's a lot of good stuff you can do. You understand what it's like to be targeted, to be got at. I saw the way people reacted to you in that hall, the way they listened when you spoke. You've got respect in this community. Have you ever thought of going into local politics?

DUWAYNE: What?

BRIAN: Local politics. Work for your community. Real work where people come to you about things that matter to them.

DUWAYNE: Aren't you supposed to be neutral, not party political, in your situation?

BRIAN: I'm not that queen. But anyway, I'm nearly out of the Met, Duwayne. It's about to happen. Now listen. There's gonna be two vacancies in Lewisham. You know Lewisham. They know you. You interested in standing for selection?

DUWAYNE: It's a fantasy.

BRIAN: Doesn't need to be. You can do it.

DUWAYNE: The ragamuffin?

BRIAN: Where? I don't see any ragamuffin. I see a proud, presentable, honest man who's fought a long and hard battle against racism amongst the lowest and highest in the land. I see a man with passion and conviction who will stand up for others, all others. I see someone who could have succumbed, crumbled, fallen, stopped. But you didn't. You continued all these years to fight, to resist, to win. Great things will come your way, Duwayne. I know it!

SCENE 20

The two policemen move around the stage making out they are many different people. They are all very senior policemen. DUWAYNE is standing bemused, watching all the activity.

SENIOR POLICEMAN 1: Councillor Brooks, may I congratulate you on your victory in the election

SENIOR POLICEMAN 2: Councillor Brooks, I was very impressed by your speech on Stop and Search.

SENIOR POLICEMAN 3: Councillor Brooks, we would like to invite you to sit on the Stop and Search committee. We would very much value your insight.

SENIOR POLICEMAN 4: Councillor, would you be interested in sitting on the Police Reference Group.

SENIOR POLICEMAN 5: We would value your help with young people,

SENIOR POLICEMAN 6: on engagement

SENIOR POLICEMAN 7: on diversity

SENIOR POLICEMAN 8: you could come on patrol, see how we do things

SENIOR POLICEMAN 9: talk to people

SENIOR POLICEMAN 10: see what they say

SENIOR POLICEMAN 11: advise us

SENIOR POLICEMAN 12: advise us

SENIOR POLICEMAN 13: advise us.

SENIOR POLICEMAN 14: Sorry to hear you lost your seat, Duwayne.

SENIOR POLICEMAN 15: We still want you

SENIOR POLICEMAN 16: We still need you.

SENIOR POLICEMAN 17: Your advice is invaluable.

SENIOR POLICEMAN 18: Duwayne. Do you think you would mind coming along to the College of Police. We have these sessions with superintendents, the most senior police. Just small groups, where you sit with them, they ask you what you think. They tell you what they think. We would really appreciate it.

SCENE 21

DUWAYNE is sitting in a circle with the Senior Police.

SENIOR POLICEMAN 19: Duwayne, this dialogue is so important. It's incredibly useful to tell you about our stresses, the stress of being a policeman, the effects on family life.

DUWAYNE: It's incredibly interesting for me to hear it from you.

SENIOR POLICEMAN 20: Do you think I could ask you

DUWAYNE: Ask anything.

SENIOR POLICEMAN 20: Well, what I really want to know is, what was it like for you, when it happened, how did you feel, what went through your mind, what did you think. Do you mind me asking?

DUWAYNE: What did I think? What did I feel? No I don't mind. Well, I ran to the phone. There was a phone near by. I rang 999.........

BLACK.

Music starts quietly.

VOICE OVER: 3 January 2012. Two men have been convicted of the racist murder of black teenager Stephen Lawrence, eighteen years after he was stabbed to death near a bus station in South East London. Gary Dobson and David Norris were found guilty by an Old Bailey jury in a trial based on forensic evidence

Music continues loudly.

THE HALF LIFE OF LOVE

DEVISED AND DEVELOPED WITH SATINDER KUMAR

Characters

EAMONN

ALEX

CONNOR

The Half Life of Love – UK was first performed 16 May 2016 at Rialto Theatre, Brighton with the following cast:

Jack Klaff	EAMONN
Paul Moriarty	ALEX
Laurence Bown	CONNOR

Director	Martin Dickinson
Production Manager	Paul Debreczeny
Designer	Sharon Davey

The Half Life of Love – USA was First performed at the Verona Studio, Salem Oregon 6 May 2017 with the following cast:

Raissa Fleming	EAMONN
Pamela Bilderbeck	ALEX
Barry Sexton	CONNOR

Director	Seth Allen
Production Manager	Katie Leigh

SCENE 1

It is 10 o'clock at night. ALEX is sitting in his armchair in a comfortable flat. He is listening to classical music and he is slowly sipping a glass of red wine as he reads a book and listens to the music. ALEX is 59 years old.

The doorbell suddenly rings. ALEX looks up surprised and the doorbell immediately goes again. He goes to the door and looks through the keyhole, gasps and opens the door.

CONNOR walks in. He is 17. They stand looking at each other.

ALEX: My God! I can't believe it. Connor? Is it you!

CONNOR: It sure is!

ALEX: My God!

CONNOR: You already said.

ALEX: But I just, my God. Look at you!

CONNOR: Look at you!

ALEX: Me? I'm just the same, but you...

CONNOR: What? Is there something... is it, what?

ALEX: It's just so, amazing to see you!

CONNOR: Good to see you too.

ALEX: What's, why are you, I mean, what are you doing here?

CONNOR: Can I come in?

ALEX: Of course. Come, come sit. Are you hungry? Some wine?

CONNOR: Wine?

ALEX: You're allowed now, aren't you, my God, I mean, how old are you now?

CONNOR: 'Course I'm allowed. And even if I wasn't, it wouldn't mean I

ALEX: Well, it might not, but, I wouldn't, anyway, of course, let me get you a glass. Come sit down.

He gets a glass and fills it with wine. He passes it to CONNOR who downs it almost in one. ALEX is a bit surprised.

ALEX: Were you thirsty, or... Do you want some water?

CONNOR: No. I just, I suppose I should've sipped it. It's not my normal drink.

ALEX: What is?

CONNOR: This and that.

ALEX: Connor. My God, I just am, I mean, I really don't know what to say. Does Eamonn know you're here?

CONNOR: No!

ALEX: No, I suppose he would've

CONNOR: Yes. He would've.

ALEX: But you, I mean. God.

CONNOR: It's ok, Alex.

ALEX: Yes, of course. It is. It's great.

CONNOR: I can go, if it's really bothering you.

ALEX: It's not. How can you think that? It's just, such a surprise. I mean, it's five years now.

CONNOR: I don't have to stay.

ALEX: No, I said, it's amazing

CONNOR: I could've gone to my girlfriend.

ALEX: You've got a girlfriend now? That's great. What's her name?

CONNOR: She's twenty seven.

ALEX: Really!

CONNOR: Yeah!

ALEX: What do you mean, you could've gone to her? You mean, you have to go, you need to go somewhere? I mean, what about Eamonn. Can't you just

CONNOR: I can, I can. It's cool.

ALEX: Go home. Do you have to

CONNOR: No, I said, it's not a problem.

ALEX: What? Did you leave home, or did he

CONNOR: He didn't kick me out.

ALEX: Did he?

CONNOR: No.

ALEX: But

CONNOR: I left.

ALEX: left? As in, ran away from home?

CONNOR: No. I'm not seven.

ALEX: How old are you?

CONNOR: Twenty.

ALEX: Twenty! Never. I mean, let me think, ahm, you were twelve and that was, ahh, 2009. You're

CONNOR: Well almost. I'm seventeen. Nearly eighteen.

ALEX: Seventeen.

CONNOR: Nearly eighteen.

ALEX: Why'd you run?

CONNOR: I said, I didn't run away.

ALEX: Yeah, sure, so why did you?

CONNOR: I couldn't take it anymore with him.

ALEX: With Eamonn?

CONNOR: Yeah. Course. There's no-one else,

ALEX: He doesn't have anyone else?

CONNOR: No.

ALEX: What about

CONNOR: He left.

ALEX: Fin left?

CONNOR: No.

ALEX: What happened to him?

CONNOR: He…

ALEX: What?

CONNOR: Got rid of him.

ALEX: What the hell does that mean?

CONNOR: What do you do with an unwanted cat?

ALEX: He's not a cat.

CONNOR: Well he did the human of what you'd do to a cat.

ALEX: What the hell does that mean?

CONNOR: You're repeating yourself.

ALEX: What did he do, Connor?

CONNOR: He gave him back.

ALEX: To your parents?

CONNOR: Don't be stupid.

ALEX: To whom then?

CONNOR: Social services.

ALEX: So where is he now?

CONNOR: Foster home. Well he was. He's left now. He's on his own.

ALEX: In a flat?

CONNOR: Hostel.

ALEX: He's living in a hostel?

CONNOR: Yeah.

ALEX: Bloody hell.

CONNOR: I wish I could.

ALEX: You want to live in a hostel?

CONNOR: Why not? You think it's for losers?

ALEX: No. No, of course not.

CONNOR: Well you say it like, hostel, as if it's just for

ALEX: No, I'm not. It's, I know it's great for people who want their independence. I know that. It's just

CONNOR: He's alright.

ALEX: Do you see him?

CONNOR: Yeah.

ALEX: What? A lot?

CONNOR: About twice a year.

ALEX: Is that all?

CONNOR: Well

ALEX: When did he leave?

CONNOR: He didn't leave.

ALEX: Well, when was he pushed?

CONNOR: About three years now.

ALEX: Three years ago! God!

CONNOR: Yeah.

ALEX: Why?

CONNOR: Drugs.

ALEX: Drugs? Fin?

CONNOR: Yeah.

ALEX: Jesus.

CONNOR: Yeah.

ALEX: Jesus! I'm, really sorry to

CONNOR: Look, I gotta go.

ALEX: You've got to go? Really?

CONNOR: Yeah, I can't hang about.

ALEX: But

CONNOR: My girlfriend's waiting.

ALEX: Your twenty seven year old girlfriend?

CONNOR: Yeah.

ALEX: Where's she waiting?

CONNOR: She's just waiting.

ALEX: Is she downstairs? Tell her to come up.

CONNOR: No.

ALEX: Ok. So. Wow, what can I say, it was really good to see you, Connor.

CONNOR: Alex.

ALEX: Yeah.

CONNOR: Do you think you could

ALEX: What?

CONNOR: I mean, I haven't got

ALEX: What?

CONNOR: It's ok.

ALEX: Tell me, Connor. You could always talk to me, couldn't you?

CONNOR: Yeah.

ALEX: What is it then? What do you need? Money?

CONNOR: Yeah.

ALEX: You need money?

CONNOR: Yeah.

ALEX: Why? What do you need it for?

CONNOR: What do you mean? I just, need it.

ALEX: Yeah, you need it, but, for what?

CONNOR: I just need it!

ALEX: For, for what? For drugs?

CONNOR: What?

ALEX: Do you? Is that what it's all about?

CONNOR: I thought I could always come to you.

ALEX: You can. You could.

CONNOR: That's what you always said, remember?

ALEX: Yes, I remember. I remember very well. I said it five years ago when I last saw you, I said, you can always come to me. But you never did.

CONNOR: It's alright.

ALEX: Now you come. Five years later. And suddenly here you are, out of the blue. And I see what you've really come for is money. For drugs.

CONNOR: Yeah. Ok. I knew it wouldn't work.

ALEX: What wouldn't? That you would just turn up and I'd just take out a wad and off you'd go and find the first pusher. Is that what isn't working?

CONNOR: Yeah. Anyone connected to my dad isn't gonna give me apeshit!

ALEX: Apeshit? What American programme did you hear that on?

CONNOR: It's fine.

ALEX: No it's not. It's not fine. I see you turn up, seventeen, pretending to be twenty, pretending to someone who wouldn't take two seconds to work out it's a lie. So what does that mean? One, that you say that all the time and your brain is so addled that you don't realise to whom you are speaking. Or two, that you really want me to know that you're

CONNOR: I'm fine.

ALEX: Not fine. One or two?

CONNOR: There's not just two.

ALEX: What's three then?

CONNOR: Three is,

ALEX: Yeah?

CONNOR: Three is, I'm outa here.

ALEX: Why are you talking like an American?

CONNOR: Don't worry. See you again in a few years, yeah?

ALEX: No, don't go like this. Come and sit down. Tell me, is there a girl waiting downstairs?

CONNOR: What if there is?

ALEX: It's just rude, that's all. I wouldn't want to keep her waiting.

CONNOR: She's not downstairs.

ALEX: So, can you stay a bit?

CONNOR: What for?

ALEX: Is it really only money that's made you come?

CONNOR: You were always so full of shit.

ALEX: Is that how you remember me?

CONNOR: Yeah.

ALEX: I remember you very differently.

CONNOR: A sweet little boy.

ALEX: Yes. A sweet little boy. A boy who always tried so hard.

CONNOR: Loser, huh.

ALEX: Tried so hard to get someone to love him.

CONNOR: You say I sound American. What American shit is this? Poor boy, looking for a daddy to lurve him.

ALEX: Playing football, running, always running, never walking. Always wanting picnics. Let's have a picnic,

you'd always say. Tuna sandwiches. Let's have tuna
sandwiches.

CONNOR: Motherhood and apple pie, hey. What could be cuter?

ALEX: Do you still love tuna sandwiches?

CONNOR: No. Nowadays my taste has become more sophisticated.

ALEX: Jam sandwiches?

CONNOR: Yeah, but raspberry.

They both smile.

ALEX: I can't tell you how good it is to see you. You've grown,
you've become a

CONNOR: Man?

ALEX: Boy-man.

CONNOR: Boy-man?

ALEX: Good-looking!

CONNOR: Yeah? Really?

ALEX: Oh yes. Really.

CONNOR: Still fancy me?

ALEX: Connor! Come on. That's,

CONNOR: Not funny?

ALEX: Not called for.

CONNOR: So, not funny?

ALEX: No. Not funny.

CONNOR: My dad would have

ALEX: He wouldn't've thought it was funny.

CONNOR: He didn't think many things were funny.

ALEX: No.

CONNOR: He'd laugh if you fell.

ALEX: If you tripped

CONNOR: The time you slipped

ALEX: You mean the swimming pool?

CONNOR: Yeah.

ALEX: Bloody hell.

CONNOR: It was funny.

ALEX: For you lot. Killing yourselves laughing.

CONNOR: Your face!

ALEX: My arse!

CONNOR: Oh yeah, I remember that bruise

ALEX: How did you see it?

CONNOR: When you showed my dad.

ALEX: You shouldn't've

CONNOR: *(Laughs.)*

ALEX: He prodded it.

CONNOR: I'm too young to hear about such things, thank you very much.

ALEX: The bruise. He prodded the bruise. You don't prod bruises.

CONNOR: He liked to prod. In fact, he was a right prodder, wasn't he. He'd always bloody prod. Splinter in your finger, prod. Cut on your arm, prod. Varruca. Prod.

ALEX: Varruca?

CONNOR: Yeah. Remember when I couldn't go swimming that time

ALEX: Oh yes. What a bloody fuss you made.

CONNOR: I was only ten.

ALEX: I know.

CONNOR: You said I was sweet.

ALEX: To me you were. To other kids, people, you were

CONNOR: No, don't say it.

ALEX: What? Velociraptor?

CONNOR: That's not fair!

ALEX: You were though. You and Fin. My God, the way you both behaved, the way you, do you remember the way the two of you banged into those two, kept banging and banging

CONNOR: Lesbians

ALEX: in your

CONNOR: Dodgems

ALEX: Bumper cars. Why are you so…. Anyway, what's this about lesbians.

CONNOR: They were! Don't you remember? All butch. We laughed.

ALEX: I didn't laugh.

CONNOR: You laughed. We laughed how they went, if you can't look after your children, I'll knock your fucking block off!

ALEX: They didn't!

CONNOR: Something like that.

ALEX: The two of you were vicious. Bloody hell. I remember watching you in the gardens from my flat, how the two of you made those little

CONNOR: rich kids

ALEX: lives a bloody

CONNOR: rich spoilt kids.

ALEX: Anyway.

CONNOR: Rich, farty, pimply, spoilt kids.

ALEX: Connor. You know what you sound like?

CONNOR: We didn't like being called velociraptors.

ALEX: They didn't call

CONNOR: No you.

ALEX: Well

CONNOR: Is that a sorry?

ALEX: If you want. But, why did you, anyway, do you still

CONNOR: It's not like that now.

ALEX: What is it like now?

CONNOR: What do you mean, now?

ALEX: What's it like, now, with others, I mean.

CONNOR: It's not like that.

ALEX: You, got friends?

CONNOR: Yeah. Course.

ALEX: And your girlfriend.

CONNOR: Yeah.

ALEX: What's her name?

CONNOR: Chris.

ALEX: Chris. Chrissy?

CONNOR: Just Chris.

ALEX: What does she do, Chris?

CONNOR: What do you mean?

ALEX: What work?

CONNOR: She…

ALEX: What?

CONNOR: Why do you wanna know?

ALEX: Well,

CONNOR: What does it matter?

ALEX: It doesn't matter, it's just

CONNOR: It's got nothing to do with you, what she does.

ALEX: Why's it a secret?

CONNOR: She's, not working now.

ALEX: Ok. She did though?

CONNOR: Work?

ALEX: What you hiding, Connor?

CONNOR: What?

ALEX: You're being so evasive. I mean, I'm not asking for the code to the Queen's safe, her jewels.

CONNOR: Shit. I always hated that about you.

ALEX: What did you hate?

CONNOR: That sarcasm.

ALEX: Was I being sarcastic?

CONNOR: The queen's jewels!

ALEX: What's wrong with Chrissy?

CONNOR: Chris. I told you.

ALEX: Is there something wrong with her?

CONNOR: She's fit.

ALEX: Fit? As in, she can run a mile.

CONNOR: Duh!

ALEX: Ok. She's fit. So, that begs the question

CONNOR: What?

ALEX: What the hell's she doing with a seventeen year old kid?

CONNOR: You mean me?

ALEX: No, I mean…. Yes, I mean you.

CONNOR: You think I'm not fit?

ALEX: I told you you're good looking.

CONNOR: So why wouldn't she want to be with me?

Pause ALEX is exasperated.

ALEX: Has your dad met her?

CONNOR: You're joking, right?

ALEX: So, who are you protecting, him or her?

CONNOR: You're full of shit, Alex.

ALEX: Both?

CONNOR: I don't have to protect him. Did he protect me?

ALEX: Yes.

CONNOR: What! Have you forgotten? How short is your
    memory? Do you really…. you can't've…… it's the red
    wine. You sit here, in your chair. It's an old man chair.
    How old are you, Alex! Eighty? You sit, with your wine,
    and your book and your old man chair. And there's this
    old man music coming out. Why are you so old? When did
    you become… you used to be, you were young, when I …

ALEX: Jesus Connor. I'm not even sixty.

CONNOR: No, you're seventy. You're eighty. You're an old
    man. An old fart. An old geezer. A shit house.

ALEX: Why are you so angry?

CONNOR: I'm not angry. I'm just, disappointed. I'm
    disappointed in you, Alex. You said I could come

whenever I wanted to. You said that. I bet you don't even remember now. You don't, do you? I bet you've got Alzheimers. You do, don't you. You've got Alzheimers now. You think I'm just making it up. But you said I could come, whenever...

ALEX: I know I said that.

CONNOR: But you didn't mean it.

ALEX: Of course I did, Connor. I do.

CONNOR: And then I come and you don't even remember.

ALEX: Of course I remember.

CONNOR: So how can you...

ALEX: I haven't forgotten.

CONNOR: But you said

ALEX: I know what happened, Connor. It's not something I'd ever forget.

CONNOR: She doesn't work.

ALEX: What? Oh you mean Chrissy, sorry, Chris.

CONNOR: She's never worked.

ALEX: Never?

CONNOR: She had kids.

ALEX: Really?

CONNOR: Yeah. You got something against

ALEX: She still has, or

CONNOR: No. Took 'em away.

ALEX: Took them away? Them? How many's them?

CONNOR: Two, or, three. Something.

ALEX: And she's, twenty seven.

CONNOR: Something like that.

ALEX: Jesus.

CONNOR: It's alright, you know.

ALEX: Yeah?

CONNOR: Hmm. Absolutely.

ALEX: Absolutely.

CONNOR: Why are you

ALEX: What?

CONNOR: Repeating. Everything I say.

Pause.

ALEX: It's my fault.

CONNOR: No, it's his.

ALEX: His?

CONNOR: Why do you say it's yours?

ALEX: I'm an adult. I knew right from the beginning what he was like. What it was like for you and Fin.

CONNOR: No you didn't.

ALEX: I didn't want to, I thought I'd make it, you know just by being around, it would make a difference. I'd be able to

CONNOR: Protect?

ALEX: Help.

CONNOR: You did help. All the time. He was always dumping us on you. Going off for weekends… or bringing people

ALEX: I know.

CONNOR: you were always, he'd phone you, please get Connor from school

ALEX: He's cracked somebody's head open and

CONNOR: Thrown out, yeah.

ALEX: Or that time you had that bike accident and

CONNOR: He phoned you

ALEX: As I was about to start my class. Can you get Connor. I can't, I'm too busy, up in London, can't do it, meetings. And of course I went. I've got to go, I said to the administrator, he's hurt himself. Why don't they just get an ambulance, she shouted as I ran through the door.

CONNOR: You bought me an ice cream

ALEX: You weren't that bad.

CONNOR: A triple choc

ALEX: I had one too.

CONNOR: You were always on a diet.

ALEX: I tried.

CONNOR: You're looking ok.

ALEX: You think so?

CONNOR: Yeah. Definitely.

ALEX: Too much red wine.

CONNOR: And ice cream?

ALEX: No, I leave that alone now.

CONNOR: Chocolates.

ALEX: I shouldn't.

CONNOR: I like Mars bars.

ALEX: Yeah? You used to like those malteser things.

CONNOR: Fin liked those.

ALEX: I can't believe you don't... you were so close, always together, always doing the same thing. I can't think of you without him. It seems so, wrong.

CONNOR: Well

ALEX: I mean how can you have just let him go. I can't understand it.

CONNOR: You think I had a choice?

ALEX: It's called fighting for something.

CONNOR: Fighting? Against Dad? You've forgotten what it was like.

ALEX: No I haven't.

CONNOR: You don't remember how he

ALEX: I remember. Believe me, I remember.

CONNOR: So how can you say?

ALEX: But he was your brother!

CONNOR: He became a stranger.

ALEX: What?

CONNOR: He wasn't there. I knew he was taking stuff.

ALEX: Heavy stuff?

CONNOR: Not at the beginning.

ALEX: How did he

CONNOR: He started pushing him away.

ALEX: Who?

CONNOR: Dad. He'd want to hug him.

ALEX: Really

CONNOR: Yeah. All the time.

ALEX: Hugging him.

CONNOR: Yeah. Shit like that.

ALEX: What did he say?

CONNOR: Fuck off.

ALEX: Your dad told him to fuck off because he wanted to hug him!

CONNOR: Yeah.

ALEX: He hated anything, girlie. Anything that was, feminine. That's what he liked about Fin, that he was always so macho. He used to say, he's a real man's man, even though he was a boy at the time. He was proud of, you know, the way he climbed, played rugby.

CONNOR: Kicked people.

ALEX: Well I'm not sure about that but… it was different with you, wasn't it. You were

CONNOR: You saying I was girlie?

ALEX: No! But you and Fin were different. You, it wasn't rugby with you, was it? It wasn't rough and tumble

CONNOR: I was rough and tumble

ALEX: Yeah, yeah, of course, but… Look I'm not saying you were girlie. Stop being so ridiculous. But there is big macho boy thing, and there is ordinary. And Fin was that. And you were, the other.

CONNOR: Fin was just the same as me.

ALEX: Yes, you fought. You both fought. But he was, oh for Christ's sake. This is getting silly. All I'm saying is he wasn't the huggy type. You might've been

CONNOR: I wasn't

ALEX: When you were young

CONNOR: Never. I never wanted to hug my dad.

ALEX: Oh Connor. You did. And me. You were always hugging me.

CONNOR: I wasn't. You just want to remember that. I wasn't a poof.

ALEX: Oh for God's sake! Look, let's just

CONNOR: No, let's not. Are you saying you thought I was a poof.

ALEX: I'm not even going to dignify that with an answer.

CONNOR: Did you? Did you think I was gonna grow up to be a poof? Tell me, I really want to know.

ALEX: Connor, you might want to live in the 50s but the word nowadays is gay.

CONNOR: I know.

ALEX: So, use it for fuck's sake!

CONNOR: Gay.

ALEX: Thank you.

CONNOR: I was never gay.

ALEX: What's the matter with you? Your dad's gay. I'm gay. What's the problem?

CONNOR: That.

ALEX: Because of me.

CONNOR: Both of, all of you.

ALEX: Nobody's going to make you gay.

CONNOR: They fucking better not try.

ALEX: Christ.

CONNOR: I better go.

ALEX: Maybe.

CONNOR: So, you gonna give me some money?

ALEX: I still haven't had an answer, Connor. No, I'm not going to give you money for drugs. Sorry. Come back in two years when you're clean ok. Then I'll be pleased to take you out for a meal, buy you some clothes. Put a book in your hand.

CONNOR: It's not for drugs.

ALEX: Yes I know you take me for an eighty year old who doesn't know his twitter from his twit. But this old geezer is not a fucking fool.

CONNOR: Oh piss off, Alex. What sort of a cunt is it anyway who would fuck my father!

ALEX: Connor! How dare you! That is absolutely, outrageous. I can't, what, I just, bloody hell!

As he speaks CONNOR goes to the door, opens it and slams it as he leaves.

ALEX runs after him.

ALEX: Get back here this instant! Do you hear!

Off stage.

CONNOR: Fuck off!

ALEX goes out after him. Off stage we hear.

ALEX: Don't you, how dare, just you

ALEX brings him back holding onto his ear.

CONNOR: Oww! Let go!

ALEX pushes him into a chair.

CONNOR: Bloody ear. Christ.

ALEX takes a large gulp of wine.

CONNOR: Why'd you grab my ear?

ALEX doesn't reply. Drinks more.

CONNOR: You think it comes off? Bloody doesn't. Did you know that? Not detachable you know. You don't put the good ears on, each morning. Which ones should I wear today?

ALEX: Shut up, Connor.

CONNOR: The good ones, or the everyday ones.

ALEX: Just keep quiet.

CONNOR: Like a shirt. Or a pair of trousers. Or shoes.

ALEX: Christ Connor.

CONNOR: You hurt me!

ALEX: Good.

CONNOR: Good? You a sadist now, are you?

ALEX: Yes. Good.

CONNOR: I read about people like you.

ALEX: Good.

CONNOR: People who tie up other people and do all sorts of things to them, put them in black sacks and suck oranges

ALEX: Oranges?

CONNOR: And then beat them, and women in black boots with really high heels, and handcuffs, and

ALEX: Jesus

CONNOR: with whips. You gonna bring out your whip now, Alex?

ALEX: Yeah. I am. Just gonna get it. Hold on here.

CONNOR: No!

ALEX: Oh shut up Connor!

CONNOR: I'm not gonna play your games. I don't like things like that. I'm straight. Straight as a die.

ALEX: You're so bloody stupid. When did you get so stupid?

CONNOR: It's my parents.

ALEX: Your father's so middle fucking class he probably still gets his glassware from the Conran shop.

CONNOR: What? Where's that?

ALEX: Oh God. I am bloody getting old.

CONNOR: He gets them from Tesco's. Actually.

ALEX: Yes, he bloody would.

CONNOR: Anyway, that's not who I mean.

ALEX: whom. Whom do you mean?

CONNOR: My parents. He's not my

ALEX: He is your dad. Has been since you were five.

CONNOR: By name. By official forms. According to social services.

ALEX: He took you in. Looked after you. Put a roof over your head, a teddy in your bed. Tried to love you.

CONNOR is hurt, doesn't respond.

ALEX: I mean, look fuck Connor, I don't mean you're unlovable. That's not … it's him. He tried but

CONNOR: Chris loves me.

ALEX: He's incapable

CONNOR: He's fucking, it's him, not me.

ALEX: his personality

CONNOR: I wasn't… it's not that I …

ALEX: You were fine. You were, lovely.

CONNOR: Yeah.

ALEX: Sweet. Lovely. Honestly.

CONNOR: Yeah.

ALEX: I always liked you. Loved you.

CONNOR: We got on.

ALEX: Yeah. Course. We played football.

CONNOR: You took me swimming. Picnics.

ALEX: You loved picnics.

CONNOR: Tuna

ALEX: Yeah.

CONNOR: He hated me.

ALEX: Who? Eamonn? No!

CONNOR: He loved Fin.

ALEX: Both the same. He loved you both.

CONNOR: You know he loved Fin. Say he loved Fin.

ALEX: Course he did. But not only

CONNOR: Only. He never... he used to look at me, with this
    look, this look that said you little piece of shit.

ALEX: What?! No. What rubbish.

CONNOR: You little piece of shit. That's what the look said.
    And then that's what his mouth said.

ALEX: He said that? When?

CONNOR: When I was eight.

ALEX: He was joking. You know how he used to

CONNOR: He wasn't joking.

ALEX: His 'sense of humour'!

CONNOR: This wasn't

ALEX: What had you done?

CONNOR: Done?

ALEX: Yes. What had you done? You must have done
    something for him to say... it's not the sort of thing
    someone says to an eight year old.

CONNOR: I didn't say nothing.

ALEX: Anything. You must have.

CONNOR: I was only joking. Can't he take a joke!

ALEX: A joke to... what joke?

CONNOR: Fin! I was joking with Fin.

ALEX: What did you say?

CONNOR: I didn't mean it. For Christ sake

ALEX: Yes

CONNOR: Jesus.

ALEX: You going to tell me?

CONNOR: I was eight. I was jealous.

ALEX: and you said

CONNOR: Be careful. He loves you so much, one night he's
    gonna come fuck you.

ALEX: Christ!

CONNOR: Eight. I didn't even know what fuck meant.

ALEX: Silly arse.

CONNOR: Don't call me that!

ALEX: Not you.

CONNOR: Who? Fin?

ALEX: Don't be daft.

CONNOR: Ok. I see

ALEX: Fucking arse. Had no fucking idea how he was, the damage, destroying you.

CONNOR: I shouldn't'a said.

ALEX: No. You shouldn't've.

CONNOR: I was jealous.

ALEX: Connor?

CONNOR: Yeah.

ALEX: What's going to happen to you?

CONNOR: I'm alright. I'm fine. I've got Chris. She's …

ALEX: Mmm.

CONNOR: She's

ALEX: Yeah.

CONNOR: She needs me.

ALEX: She needs you?

CONNOR: Yeah. First person to ever need me.

ALEX: Fin needed you.

CONNOR: No, he needed dad.

ALEX: Why does Chris need you? She's twenty seven. I would've thought

CONNOR: I'm not a child with her. I don't want picnics and tuna sandwiches with her.

ALEX: What do you want with her?

CONNOR: I look after her. Find places to, food. I take care, you know.

ALEX: Jesus.

CONNOR: She's really funny. She makes me laugh.

ALEX: Really?

CONNOR: God, yeah. She's this amazing mimic. You should see how she mimics all these people.

ALEX: Which people?

CONNOR: People. People who just walk past, pretend you don't exist. Or the ones that say, are you alright? Can I get you a sandwich? No, you fucking arsehole. Just give me some money!

ALEX: She begs.

CONNOR: Not all the time.

ALEX: You beg? In the street?

CONNOR: She was selling stuff.

ALEX: What stuff?

CONNOR: Big Issue for a while

ALEX: Big Issue's good.

CONNOR: Yeah, isn't it. It's really good. Good stuff inside. Have you ever read

ALEX: No.

CONNOR: But you've bought it? Given money?

ALEX: You beg on the street.

CONNOR: No, not really.

ALEX: Does Eamonn know?

CONNOR: No. Well, just this once

ALEX: What?

CONNOR: He,

ALEX: saw you?

CONNOR: Crossed the street.

ALEX: He saw you and crossed the street.

CONNOR: Might've been coincidence.

ALEX: Yes.

CONNOR: He doesn't know Chris.

ALEX: You've never introduced

CONNOR: Can you imagine it? Me bringing her into his home

ALEX: Your home.

CONNOR: Saying, this is my dad.

ALEX: No.

CONNOR: You can't. Can you?

ALEX: No.

CONNOR: I mean, hey Chris, meet my dad!

ALEX begins to laugh.

(Mimics posh accent.) How do you do, Miss. How lovely to meet you. Any friend of my dear boy is a friend of mine!

ALEX really laughs.

Come and sit down. I have prepared a lovely tea with scones and raspberry jam. And look, here is some beautiful organic double cream that I churned myself this morning.

ALEX: From my free range cow in the backyard, lolling happily alongside my free range chickens. And then I'll make dinner, vegetarian of course, with my organic butternut squash

CONNOR: that I have reared single handedly.

ALEX: Do you rear butternut squash?

CONNOR: Course.

ALEX: I'm impressed you know the word churn.

CONNOR: You taught it to me. That bedtime book you used to

ALEX: Oh yes.

CONNOR: You see, I have had some education.

ALEX: You're not stupid, Connor.

CONNOR: Nah. Bright as a, newly minted pound coin.

ALEX: You never brought friends home.

CONNOR: Fin tried once.

ALEX: You mean

CONNOR: That girl. Sharon or Tracy or Fernando

ALEX: Not Fernando.

CONNOR: You would have thought he'd been woken by banging headboards, rather than a, look at my football cards while we grab some juice and maybe a banana. You tried to calm him down. They're twelve, Eamonn, you shouted. I won't have any stuff going

ALEX: he didn't say stuff

CONNOR: on under my roof

ALEX: They're not doing anything

CONNOR: while he lives in this house

ALEX: not stuff, it was, what did he say?

CONNOR: fucking

ALEX: No. He didn't

CONNOR: Shagging

ALEX: I can't remember

CONNOR: What the fuck. Anyway, it was the last time.

ALEX: Except what he did to me later.

CONNOR: What?

ALEX: Interfering!

CONNOR: He didn't like interfering.

ALEX: I'm not interfering, Eamonn. For Christ sake. Keep your hair on.

CONNOR: That would have done it.

ALEX: Mm.

CONNOR: Was that the first time?

ALEX: When he ....

CONNOR: Was it?

ALEX: Yeah.

CONNOR: Why didn't you walk out then?

ALEX: What?

CONNOR: Why didn't you, Alex?

ALEX: I should've.

CONNOR: You looked up

ALEX: From the floor

CONNOR: into our eyes

ALEX: You were watching.

CONNOR: Why didn't you hit him back?

ALEX: You think I should've

CONNOR: Course. You gotta hit back. You gotta

ALEX: Yeah, me. The fighter.

CONNOR: We wanted you to

ALEX: Then you left.

CONNOR: We went to bed.

ALEX: I'm not a fighter.

CONNOR: He's not a fighter, Fin said.

ALEX: Oh for God's sake. You think it's right? Hit me and I'll hit you back. Is that what's needed? Is that what life's all about? Isn't there enough of it in this life? Do I have to add to it? Do I have to be macho, is that the only way I can get respect?

CONNOR: You and Jesus Christ. Turn the other cheek.

ALEX: And what's so bloody wrong with that?

CONNOR: The baddies always win. That's what's wrong.

> *Pause.*

I don't remember Fin ever crying before then.

ALEX: Fin cried? Because of what he did to me?

CONNOR: I don't think so.

ALEX: Because I just took it?

CONNOR: Maybe.

ALEX: What then?

CONNOR: It just all seemed hopeless, suddenly.

ALEX: He apologised. Said he'd never do it again. Swore, he'd never do it again. Cried.

> *Pause.*

CONNOR: It's not as if you were bad looking.

ALEX: Thanks

CONNOR: Bit short but. You were fatter.

ALEX: comfort eating.

CONNOR: Now you drink too much.

ALEX: Hey! Watch it!

CONNOR: It's true, isn't it?

ALEX: No.

CONNOR: How much do you drink at night?

ALEX: Mind your own business.

CONNOR: *(Laughs.)* You can't even hold your booze.

ALEX: I never get drunk.

CONNOR: So you have one glass, do you?

ALEX: Another big macho thing? See how much I can drink.

CONNOR: I can drink a litre of cider and nobody would know nothing.

ALEX: Aren't you the big one!

CONNOR: Nobody would know nothing. I can walk straight, no slurring. I don't even notice it.

ALEX: How much are you drinking?

CONNOR: Chris can drink, my god, she really, it just doesn't even touch the sides.

ALEX: Connor! This isn't good!

CONNOR: It's amazing!

ALEX: No, it's not. It really isn't. It's really, really, not good.

CONNOR: What isn't, you mean... I know it's not good to drink. We don't drink all the time.

ALEX: You've got to see someone.

CONNOR: Like?

ALEX: Where's your social worker?

CONNOR: No, no.

ALEX: What no no?

CONNOR: Don't even, no, don't go there.

ALEX: Does she know about

CONNOR: She speaks to Dad, he says, everything's fine and dandy. Just fine and dandy.

ALEX: He's charmed her.

CONNOR: You can say that again.

ALEX: He could always bloody charm the socks off a donkey.

CONNOR: Yeah.

ALEX: That's the middle classes, mate. There's no way they'd do anything to a charming, articulate, knows all the right words, so caring, so difficult for him, poor, poor Eamonn. He's tried so hard to give those kids a life and look how they've turned out. It's so comforting that you at least, Ms Social Worker, can understand. You at least can see that I am, trying. But it's so hard for us parents of adopted children who are, damaged. That's not too strong a word, is it, to describe these children. No matter how we try, how hard we work, my God, I've given them everything. I've sacrificed, yes, I have to say it, sacrificed my life for those children. I don't have a life, I don't have relationships because no-one can understand me, can realise that the children come first. That there is nothing other than them.

What's not to believe, for Christ sake? They look at these two, velociraptors, and they look at this charming, good looking, gay, which helps because then no-one can say that they fancied the bloke, that they took his side because they fancied him, all safe, all kosher. And the equation is not equal. I can understand that. How could they think otherwise? What would make them realise the pathological nature of this bastard. When he is so fucking charming!

CONNOR: You don't like social workers, do you?

ALEX: No. I do. Some of my best friends

CONNOR: yeah!

ALEX: She labelled me malicious, you know, when I tried to confront

CONNOR: who?

ALEX: Social services, to complain, to let them know. She stuck up for him. Said I was being malicious.

CONNOR: So now you sit in your chair.

ALEX: Being not malicious.

CONNOR: Being not anything.

ALEX: Being safe. Being fine. Being happy. Enjoying myself. Enjoying my time. My wine. My music. My bookl. Me. Me. Me!

CONNOR: You should have fought back.

ALEX: Leave me alone, Connor.

CONNOR: You let him win.

ALEX: Go look after Chris. Stop telling me what I should have done.

CONNOR: He trampled on you, squashed you like an ant at a picnic. Yuck, these horrible little ants getting in the way, upsetting me, annoying me.

ALEX: And what's an ant supposed to do? It's fine when they come in an army and they destroy as they go along. But what if you are a lone ant, an ant with no-one else to walk next to you, alongside of you.

CONNOR: You weren't alone.

ALEX: What? I had you and Fin? What were you supposed to do?

CONNOR: Fight with you.

ALEX: Against your dad? Fin would never have said a word. He was so desperate for approval.

CONNOR: I was always on your side.

ALEX: And how did that help me?

CONNOR: Well I...

ALEX: What? That you looked at me with those gooey eyes, those help-me eyes. Those, pitying eyes.

CONNOR: I only pitied you once.

ALEX: Only once? That's quite an achievement.

CONNOR: When you crawled.

ALEX: What?

CONNOR: In Paris.

Pause.

ALEX: Paris.

CONNOR: We'd had

ALEX: It was good.

CONNOR: We were a family. We were on holiday. Disney land.
My God. Disneyland! Could there be anything better?

ALEX: The parades.

CONNOR: Candy floss.

ALEX: That mountain ride.

CONNOR: Space mountain!

ALEX: Fun. It was fun.

CONNOR: We laughed. Laughed and

ALEX: I don't know what made him turn.

CONNOR: Suddenly

ALEX: So sudden. And we got back and he started

CONNOR: Shouting

ALEX: Swearing.

CONNOR: At Fin.

ALEX: First it was Fin.

CONNOR: Then me.

ALEX: Leave them alone!

CONNOR: You lost it.

ALEX: I lost it. I'd kept it in and then, lost it.

I didn't see it coming.

CONNOR: You twirled.

ALEX: Like a ballet dancer? It didn't feel balletic. It felt

CONNOR: Did you see stars, like the cartoons?

ALEX: I saw the specs on the carpet, the crumbs.

CONNOR: You crawled.

ALEX: I was trying to get away.

CONNOR: You crawled away and he was kicking you and, with his feet, his shoes still on, kicking, and you crawled away.

ALEX: He could've killed me.

CONNOR: Crawling

ALEX: For Christ's sake, Connor! He was bloody killing me. What did you want me to do?

CONNOR: Nothing. Of course. Nothing. He was gonna kill you.

ALEX: What? It's not manly enough for you, is it? I should've jumped up, put out my hands, boxing, showing what a man I am. Is that it? Too much of a poof for you, was I?

CONNOR: He was gonna kill you.

ALEX: Too much of a queen? A little limp wristed, queen. Is that it? You stood there. I didn't see you putting up your fists, fighting to

CONNOR: I was twelve

ALEX: The velociraptor. Where was the velociraptor when I needed him? Huh!

CONNOR: I wanted to

ALEX: You wanted to? You wanted to come and help the crawling, pathetic

CONNOR: No, you weren't

ALEX: I was. You know it. You knew it then. You look at me now and you know it now.

CONNOR: What do you want me to say?

ALEX: The truth.

CONNOR: I was so young.

ALEX: You were twelve.

CONNOR: I was so small. So weak.

ALEX: But what did you think?

CONNOR doesn't reply.

ALEX: Tell me! Do you think I can't take it? You thought I was weak, pathetic. You felt sorry for me. I saw it. I know. It doesn't matter what you say. I know it. You thought, I don't

143

want to be like him. I never want to be a useless, weakling, pathetic, idiot

CONNOR: No!

ALEX: Funny, isn't it? You protecting me now. You don't have to. Anything you can tell me, I have told myself, and worse, I can promise you.

CONNOR: But I didn't.

ALEX: Oh yeah. There I am crawling, snivelling, snot pouring out, blood flooding the floor, Crying. Did I call out for my mother. I can't remember. I probably did.

CONNOR: It wasn't like that.

ALEX: Disgust. You felt disgust. Why don't you get up! Be a man!

CONNOR: Hatred.

ALEX: You hated me. I know. I hated myself.

CONNOR: Him! I hated him! I hated him so strongly like I'd never felt hate before. I've hated, I can tell you. Those rich kids, my parents, abandoning us, letting us go, giving us up. I've hated them. But in my whole life I've never hated as I hated him then. Because he was hurting the only grown-up in my life that I loved. But I couldn't move. I couldn't go to you. I tried to move my legs, they just wouldn't. Scared. I watched, looked, not able to move my eyes away, my legs, my arms, even my arms to block what was happening, to block the look, the blood, my ears, to block the screaming, the shouting, the blood. The blood.

And then you crawled out the door and the door closed and you had gone. You'd left us. Just left, left us there to be with him alone. How could you just leave us with him, alone. How could you do that to us?

He got a drink. He sat down on the sofa. He didn't look at us. We went to bed.

Fin said he hated him. Dad. He hated him. He didn't want to be like him. He never wanted to ... He changed after that. He seemed to move away from me too. It was as if I had done it to you too. As if I was responsible too. But I wasn't. I said to him, I said, Fin, I said. I said, Fin

And you didn't come back. You sent a card and said, you can come anytime. But how could we come? You didn't think that we couldn't come.

ALEX: Connor

CONNOR: You left, then wrote a note, then didn't think

ALEX: I was, too hurt.

CONNOR: But you're a grown up.

ALEX: Grown ups can hurt.

CONNOR: But grown ups know how to deal with hurt?

ALEX: I deal with it by doing what I'm doing. I build, I create, I form this wall where all that there is is me, me in my chair with my comforts, and nothing ever penetrates it.

CONNOR: You're safe.

ALEX: Safe and dandy.

CONNOR: Well that's good, isn't it.

ALEX: Yes. It's good.

CONNOR: Bully for you.

ALEX: Absolutely.

CONNOR: Well, now I know, I can leave you in your chair. Knowing that you're safe.

ALEX: Yes. Go. Leave me. I don't want to know about your begging, and your sleeping who knows where, and your girl friend, and her children, and the social worker. I don't want any of that in my life. It's clean, my life. And you're just going muck it up! Here, *(Grabs money from his pocket and throws it on the floor in front of CONNOR.)* Take that and go.

CONNOR: I don't want your money.

ALEX: Why? You did before. Why not now?

CONNOR: I don't want anything from you. I don't need you.

ALEX: Take the money *(He picks it up and pushes it into him.)* Take it. Take it, I said.

CONNOR: No! Leave it! Leave me alone!

ALEX: You'll take money from strangers, begging in the street. But you won't take it from me!

CONNOR: No!

ALEX: Take it!

CONNOR: No!

ALEX: Please.

CONNOR: No.

ALEX: Connor

CONNOR: What?

ALEX: Connor

CONNOR: What!

ALEX: I'm sorry.

CONNOR: What are you sorry for, Alex?

ALEX: I'm sorry I didn't try harder. I'm sorry I just walked away and forgot about you. I'm sorry I didn't challenge that social worker. I'm sorry I let one relationship scar me for ever. I'm sorry I closed my eyes and let two children be forgotten.

CONNOR looks at him for a while, then goes to him and hugs him.

ALEX is sobbing.

ALEX: You should stay here. I have an extra room.

CONNOR: I'm alright.

ALEX: No. You must stay here. I'll look after you. I will.

CONNOR: I have to look after Chris.

ALEX: She can stay here too.

CONNOR: *(Laughs.)* I don't think so!

ALEX: She can, Connor. I mean it.

CONNOR: When things break up with her, I'll come back to you, Alex. Do you think you'll be able to handle it?

ALEX: I'm knocking down that wall as we speak, Connor.

CONNOR: Ok, you know what? I'm gonna do you a favour. I'm gonna take that money. I'll be back!

He exits.

SCENE 2

It is 11pm the next evening. ALEX is sitting in his chair, focusing on the middle distance. A glass of wine next to him but untouched. Suddenly there is a ringing of the bell. He opens the door and EAMONN is standing there.

ALEX: Eamonn! What the hell are you doing here?

EAMONN: Hello Alex.

ALEX: I can't believe you're...

EAMONN: How are you?

ALEX: I...

EAMONN: Can I come in?

ALEX: What?

EAMONN: Can I?

ALEX: What are you doing here?

EAMONN: Can we discuss it indoors?

ALEX: But...

EAMONN: I won't stay long, if you don't...

ALEX: I don't think...

EAMONN: Please Alex.

ALEX: Did you see Connor?

EAMONN: I need to speak to you, Alex

ALEX: Is that why you're...

EAMONN: It won't...

ALEX: I mean, what are you...

EAMONN: Please. I'm begging you.

ALEX: But wh...

He walks in but doesn't shut the door properly behind him.

EAMONN: Thanks, Alex. Honestly just...

ALEX: One minute, Eamonn. I swear...

EAMONN: You're looking well.

ALEX: What are you doing here?

EAMONN: I've come to see you.

ALEX: At eleven at night?

EAMONN: I'm sorry. I know it's late.

ALEX: It is!

EAMONN: I am sorry, honestly Alex.

ALEX: Well I mean, barging in, at this time of night like this, I mean, honestly it's...

EAMONN: Unforgiveable.

ALEX: It is! It really is!

EAMONN: It's good to see you though. You're looking well. You've, slimmed down a lot.

Pause.

ALEX: What do you want, Eamonn?

EAMONN: How are you, Alex? Are you alright? You seem a bit...

ALEX: Edgy?

EAMONN: Well, yes.

ALEX: Edgy.

EAMONN: Well, slightly.

ALEX: And that's a wonder, is it?

EAMONN: No, no.

ALEX: Surprising?

EAMONN: Of course not.

ALEX: You beat me up. Do you even remember?

EAMONN: Of course.

ALEX: You stood over me with your children watching, and kicked me. I crawled away with you kicking me. Screaming and kicking.

EAMONN: I know.

ALEX: You know, do you?

EAMONN: It was five years ago.

ALEX: It was five minutes ago, you shithouse.

EAMONN: Maybe you could, try to let it go.

ALEX: I should let it go, should I?

EAMONN: I know it's difficult.

ALEX: You do.

EAMONN: Of course.

ALEX: You know I can let go of some things. I can let go of the image of you screaming and yelling and kicking. I can let go of those words you shouted, the sounds, the grunts. But you know what won't go? Simply won't go, as much as I *try* to let it go. What sticks like the toughest limpet holding on for dear life to a rock in a tsunami is the snivelling. The weeping, the sniffing, the gurgling. The sound of me pleading, leave me alone, don't touch me, ow, you're hurting me. Stop it, Eamonn. Stop it.

EAMONN: I, I can't forgive myself.

ALEX: Can't you?

EAMONN: It was...

ALEX: Unforgiveable?

EAMONN: Yes.

ALEX: Like coming here at eleven o'clock at night.

EAMONN: Of course it's

ALEX: More.

EAMONN: Of course.

ALEX: Jesus, Eamonn.

EAMONN: What can I say, Alex? I, can't tell you how many times I've, wanted to come, to apologise.

ALEX: Really?

EAMONN: Honestly. I felt terrible.

ALEX: Oh. I am sorry!

EAMONN: Believe me, Alex. I really did. Do.

ALEX: You managed to contain that apology for five and a half years. Well done. It obviously managed to dissipate, to be dispelled, for you to carry on so, easily.

EAMONN: It wasn't easy.

ALEX: Easy enough for you not to have to come and, you know,

EAMONN: I'm saying sorry now.

ALEX: Oh fuck!

EAMONN: I know it's

ALEX: Unforgiveable?

EAMONN: Not easy for you to…

ALEX: Jesus. What the hell do you want, Eamonn? Why have you come?

EAMONN: Connor.

ALEX: Connor! You've come about Connor.

EAMONN: He's been a terrible worry.

ALEX: Jesus Eamonn. What the fuck is going on here?

EAMONN: It's hard, Alex. I need some help.

ALEX: You need help? Yeah. You need help.

EAMONN: I'm actually, beside myself.

ALEX: Oh come on Eamonn. There's no way you'd come to me about this. I know you. What're you playing at? What's this all about?

EAMONN: I've nowhere else to turn.

ALEX: Are you kidding me? I'm the last person in the world you'd come to about your kids.

EAMONN: In the past! That's the past, Alex. You've got to believe me. I'm a different person.

ALEX: You're as likely to be different as a snake faced with a juicy mouse.

EAMONN: I'm not a snake Alex. Not anymore.

ALEX: So you're saying you were. Acknowledging your…

EAMONN: I wasn't always the, nicest.

ALEX: No you bloody weren't. You abso-bloody fucking weren't.

EAMONN: I know you're upset.

ALEX: Have you been having counselling, Eamonn? Have you been taught to say, I know you're upset. Are you going to start saying now, I hear your pain. Are you going to start fucking hearing my pain now?

EAMONN: I'm not going to say that, Alex.

ALEX: Yeah! They're clever these counsellors. Don't be too heavy, take it easy. Don't make it too obvious.

EAMONN: I haven't had counselling.

ALEX: Well you bloody should've.

EAMONN: Maybe.

ALEX: No fucking maybe.

Pause.

EAMONN: Are you going to offer me some of that wine?

ALEX goes and pours him a glass and hands it to him. He is shaking. EAMONN notices it. ALEX has a big gulp of his wine. EAMONN sips his.

EAMONN: Thank you for this,

ALEX: It's a pleasure, I'm sure.

EAMONN: Do I make you nervous?

ALEX: I always feel like this when past lovers who beat me up come calling in the middle of the night. It's the pleasant anticipation. Will they do it again?

EAMONN: Stop it, Alex. I said I'm sorry. I'm

ALEX: Filled with remorse. I know. I can see!

EAMONN: Well, maybe I was wrong. Maybe I shouldn't've come after all. I'll go. Shall I?

He gets up.

ALEX: Yes. Go.

EAMONN: Could I just have a couple more sips?

ALEX: Piss off Eamonn.

EAMONN: Shame to waste a good bottle.

ALEX: I won't waste it.

EAMONN: I mean, my glass.

ALEX: Have a sip if you bloody want one.

He sits.

EAMONN: Thank you.

ALEX: Jesus.

EAMONN: You always had a nose for good wine.

ALEX: Like I've got so much else in my life.

EAMONN: Haven't you, Alex?

They drink in silence.

EAMONN: You've lost weight. It suits you.

ALEX: Well, you know what it's like, when you're single you gotta try.

EAMONN: I know.

ALEX: Can't say the same about you.

EAMONN: Comfort eating.

ALEX: Huh!

EAMONN: No sympathy then, Alex!

ALEX laughs.

EAMONN: Wow. A laugh. That's progress.

ALEX: More a satisfying gulp of schadenfreude.

EAMONN: I've got to go to the gym.

ALEX: You always said that. You never got there.

EAMONN: It's work. It's crazy.

ALEX: Excuses, excuses.

EAMONN: You're right. I'm a lazy bugger. If it's a glass of wine or that bloody treadmill thing. Well, no competition, is there!

ALEX: You'll end up with a stroke.

EAMONN: I'm a lot more relaxed now. Not so uptight, tense all the time.

ALEX: How do you manage it? Hit a few lovers from time to time. Does that help?

EAMONN: Pespective. Priorities.

ALEX: So what's your perspective on Fin and Connor now? Now that they've left you and are so, successful. You must be proud.

EAMONN: That's why I've come here to see you. I know when to look for help. Not afraid anymore to seek it, when I need it. Not stew, you know. Like I used to.

ALEX: Stew, boil, erupt.

EAMONN: Not anymore.

ALEX: I haven't seen them for five years.

EAMONN: Apart from yesterday.

ALEX: How do you know that? Are you spying? On me or on him?

EAMONN: I knew Connor would come to you.

ALEX: He hasn't for five years.

EAMONN: You always had such a good relationship with him.

ALEX: But how did you know he came?

EAMONN: He always loved you more than me.

ALEX: Don't put this on me, Eamonn. I never tried to steal Connor away from you.

EAMONN: I never said you did. I loved them both. My boys. Connor didn't understand. He didn't realise how I felt. But he seemed to understand how you felt.

ALEX: He was always your kid. They both were, always.

EAMONN: I appreciated your being there

ALEX: Appreciated? Is that what it was? It seemed like the major cause of your resentment towards me, my being with them, being there, the relationship. You needed it, but couldn't cope with it.

EAMONN: I'm losing them, Alex. Everything I've loved is just, slipping out of my hands.

ALEX: You've only got yourself to blame.

EAMONN: Do you think I don't know that? I'm my own worst enemy. You think I don't tell myself that in the middle of the night, when I lie there in bed, alone, alone in the house. No-one there, just me and my bloody miserable thoughts. Nobody hates you as much as you do yourself in the middle of the night.

ALEX: Tell me about it.

EAMONN: Is it true of you too, Alex?

ALEX: Of course. Nobody knows the softest parts of the back to beat yourself with, the spot that feels it hardest.

EAMONN: Yeah.

Pause.

EAMONN: I am sorry. Alex, believe me. I am.

I've missed you.

ALEX: Oh yeah.

EAMONN: Honestly.

ALEX: You missed having someone to look after your kids, make sure things didn't fall apart. Oh Alex is gone. Now the kids have fucked up. All his fault.

EAMONN: I never thought it was your fault.

ALEX: Of course it wasn't!

EAMONN: I know, I know, that's what I'm saying. And it wasn't just the kids. We had something.

ALEX: You had something. You had a nanny, a parent for your kids.

EAMONN: I know.

ALEX: Fucking easy to say, I know. Isn't it?

EAMONN: Don't be so hard on me, Alex. We once meant the world to each other, remember.

ALEX: Christ, Eamonn. Are you reading true romance magazines now? What is it? Those pictures with bubbles coming out of their mouths. Oh Noeline, we meant the world to each other. I know, Hubert, I'm so sorry. But Noeline.

EAMONN: I'm really worried about Connor, Alex. What do you think? You saw him, what's your impression?

Pause.

ALEX: I don't think he's on drugs.

EAMONN: I'm sure he is.

ALEX: I mean serious ones.

EAMONN: Do you even know what marijuana is like these days? Fucks you up, makes you paranoid.

ALEX: He didn't seem paranoid to me.

EAMONN: You haven't seen him sitting on the streets, begging, with his head down

ALEX: Maybe he was hiding his face from you.

EAMONN: It's pathetic. It's embarrassing. My father thinks he...

ALEX: Your father never cared a fuck for Connor.

EAMONN: He was just protecting me.

ALEX: From your kids?

EAMONN: You know my father, he never...

ALEX: He never. That's the thing with him. He never. He never thought you should have adopted kids, any kids let alone damaged kids. He never tried to relate to those kids. Made them feel like they were baggage you had to carry around. The rubbish that you should've thrown out. Didn't even look them in the eyes. I know, because he treated me exactly the same way.

EAMONN: He's my father. Real, biological father.

ALEX: That's first class is it? As opposed to you, second class? If you were a second class father, Eamonn, it had nothing to do with you being their adopted father.

EAMONN: A second class father?

ALEX: Well what do you think you were? Doesn't your sense of perspective reach to the reality of what you were like?

EAMONN: I tried, Alex. Isn't that what one is supposed to do? You can't always succeed, but at least you try.

ALEX: Yeah, that's true, if you're talking sums, arithmetic at school, an essay. But not children's lives.

EAMONN: Not everyone can succeed. Whose fault is it that I couldn't be a good father? Is it mine? Or my father's?

ALEX: It's fucking yours! Yours!

EAMONN: So the sympathy is for the poor child who is abused. And when that poor child grows up, damaged because of everything he endured, and abuses someone else, the sympathy gets replaced by repulsion, anger, disgust. But he's still the damaged boy, only grown now, and with power that he never had when he was small. Why does the sympathy leave him so utterly?

ALEX: Because that behaviour from adults is not acceptable! And you weren't abused as a boy. You had a father who loved you. Thought you were the bees' fucking knees.

EAMONN: There's abuse and abuse. I always had to be the best. First in class, first class degree, best job for a first class company. Perfect in everything I do.

ALEX: God protect us from perfection.

EAMONN: You know what pressure it is to always be perfect.

ALEX: I never had that problem.

EAMONN: Except that I was gay. That was distinctly second class.

ALEX: Poor you! You're fifty Eamonn. When are you gonna get over being a disappointment to your father?

EAMONN: It's that look in his eyes, the way he says, how are the boys these days. Smirking. Actually you know what it is? That is schadenfreude, real schadenfreude. Your boys are a fuck up. You've made your bed, now go lie in it. If you'd had a woman like any normal man, this would never have happened. She would have borne you children and then looked after them. In the natural way. As it should be. Normal.

ALEX: I'm sure Fin in his hostel and Connor in his crap sit, wherever he manages to put his head down at night, feel very sorry for you.

EAMONN: Please don't be sarcastic, Alex. I know it's all my fault. I can't tell you how terrible I feel about Fin. I know it's time I stopped being a daddy's boy, daddy's failure, that I have to take responsibility for myself. Of course I know that! But knowing is the easy part.

ALEX: Well get some help. Go get that counselling. There are people out there who understand, who will see the sad boy and try to do something about it. For money!

EAMONN: What do you see when you look at me, Alex?

ALEX: The truth, Eamonn?

EAMONN: Yes.

ALEX: I see someone sitting in front of me who is sad and pathetic, who pretends he knows he is sad and pathetic but really, and actually, thinks he is still that first class, perfect being his father always told him he was. What me, this handsome creature, this brilliant student, this highly paid professional, a failure? Hardly! And I see someone who has managed to fuck up three perfectly good lives! And that doesn't include his own.

EAMONN: Well I asked for it, I suppose.

ALEX: You can give, but you can't take.

EAMONN: I am taking it. I'm taking it from you.

ALEX: Are you serious, Eamonn? Is this just some, joke, some come-on, some game you're playing?

EAMONN: No.

ALEX: People don't really change.

EAMONN: People can.

ALEX: But

EAMONN: People can, Alex. I have.

ALEX: I can't believe that. I just simply cannot

EAMONN: I can understand that. Once a shit. Why would you believe…

ALEX: Yes.

EAMONN: I'm not a shit anymore.

ALEX: Jesus Eamonn.

EAMONN: You've got to trust me, Alex.

ALEX: It's a fucking hard ask.

EAMONN: But sometimes the hardest things give the biggest rewards.

ALEX: Cliché, Eamonn.

EAMONN: You won't believe me but…

ALEX: What?

EAMONN: I've really missed you.

ALEX: Please!

EAMONN: Honestly. I swear! I've never felt about anyone like I did about you.

ALEX: You had some bloody horrible ways of showing it.

EAMONN: I know.

ALEX: I just can't believe I'm actually letting you speak. Bloody having you here in my flat, my own flat, and letting you say these things and not throwing you out. What the fuck's the matter with me.

EAMONN: It's not always possible to unlove.

ALEX: I hate you, Eamonn. I don't love you!

EAMONN: It carries on. It doesn't just evaporate, stop, not be. Where can that love go? It's there inside you, living. Less and less, but it carries on. It doesn't die. Haven't you read Junot Diaz ? The half life of love is forever.

ALEX: The half life of love is toxic. Poisons the insides, like a cancer. Impossible to get rid of. Nowhere to put the waste. Just have to allow it to disintegrate. But it can take a lifetime to do that. And what do I do while I wait.

EAMONN: Come back to me, Alex. I've missed you.

ALEX: Bloody hell!

EAMONN: I swear I still love you.

ALEX: Christ! What's happening to me!

EAMONN: Admit it! Alex, admit it. You've missed me.

ALEX: Yes, I bloody have! I've missed you every single bloody day since I left!

EAMONN: You see! You see! You still love me!

ALEX: Jesus Eamonn. Jesus Jesus Christ!

EAMONN: It's ok. Alex, it's ok.

ALEX: It's been so long and I've been here just sitting and thinking, that's what I seem to do and, now you're here and...

EAMONN: I am here, Alex.

ALEX: I just don't know how to feel.

EAMONN: Just remember how it used to be. How we used to feel together. How we used to be together. We were incredible.

EAMONN kisses him.

ALEX: Jesus Eamonn. What are you doing to me!

EAMONN: Don't fight it.

ALEX: I can't believe I'm doing this with you.

EAMONN: It's ok.

ALEX: I've hated you for so long and now

EAMONN: It's alright.

ALEX: I'm so weak.

EAMONN: You're not. This is right.

They kiss passionately and in the midst the door is pushed open and CONNOR stands there.

CONNOR: What are you doing?!

ALEX: I…

CONNOR: What are you doing with him?

ALEX: I don't quite…

CONNOR: You told me you hate him.

ALEX: I do. I did.

CONNOR: You lied to me.

ALEX: No, I didn't.

CONNOR: I can't trust you.

ALEX: You can trust me, Connor.

CONNOR: How can I?

ALEX: Things, change.

CONNOR: How can things change so fucking fast?

ALEX: I don't know. I can't believe it myself, but…

CONNOR: Everything you said.

ALEX: I know.

CONNOR: Why, Alex?

ALEX: Because I, he…

CONNOR: What? Because you what?

ALEX: Because I, when he, it just, I don't know.

EAMONN: Because he's weak.

ALEX: What?

EAMONN: He's weak.

ALEX: What do you mean, Eamonn? What are you saying?

EAMONN: You're weak. A weakling. Mr weaky peaky. Picky pocky. Useless Alex.

ALEX: What?

EAMONN: What? You thought I wanted you? You thought, I need you!

ALEX: But you said…?

EAMONN: I said what? That I've changed, that I'm sorry, that I missed you.

ALEX: You said…

EAMONN: I did. I said it all. Easy to say. Doesn't mean I meant one fucking measly little thing of it.

ALEX: But then, why…

EAMONN: Why? To give my boy a lesson. To educate him. Teach my son.

ALEX: A lesson?

EAMONN: A lesson in trust. Letting him know what people are like, and that you can never trust anyone.

ALEX: But you said…. Oh my God!

EAMONN: Yeah, you go to your God. All forgiving God. That's what you need now.

ALEX: It was all a…

EAMONN: Farce. Yeah.

ALEX: The things you…

EAMONN: The things I said. I deserve an Oscar, don't you think? I'm so sorry. It's, unforgiveable. Will you ever forgive me! Ha! How could you fall for it? Don't you know me at all?

ALEX: You said, change.

EAMONN: You think I'm interested in you? What? A drunken, solitary, boring little wuss. A little bloke sitting in his room listening to music and drinking red wine. All alone, thinking of a man who forgot him years ago, who only used him for his own purposes, who never could bear him much anyway even when he professed to love him. This is it, Connor. This is what life is about. You can't trust anyone because everyone is out for themselves. And you never know what anyone is thinking because they hide it from you to get what they want out of it.

ALEX: No Connor, don't listen to him.

EAMONN: Case in point.

ALEX: It's not true.

EAMONN: He'll listen to me. To his dad. Because that's what boys do. They listen to their dads.

CONNOR: Why shouldn't I listen to him? It's obvious, innit. You say something and then, there you are, snogging him. Getting all, ready to fuck him. Jesus, it's disgusting. I hate you, Alex. I really do.

ALEX: Don't hate me, Connor.

CONNOR: Why not? Why shouldn't I?

ALEX: Because I'm human. A person. They come in all shapes and sizes. Some of them are weaker than others.

EAMONN: Weak as shit.

ALEX: But don't confuse tough with strength. And don't confuse, trust

CONNOR: That's it, innit, it's trust. How can I trust you?

ALEX: This hasn't got anything to do with trust. This isn't about trust. This isn't a lesson in trust.

CONNOR: But you…

ALEX: I still love him. That's my tragedy. But it's also what makes me human. A person can't live without love. But just because I love him doesn't mean I betrayed you. I hate myself for it and sometimes love and hate get mixed up inside of you and you love the person you hate and hate the person you love. You know that, just as well as I do.

CONNOR: I don't love him. I hate him.

ALEX: You love him and wish he was a loving father and hate him because he's not.

EAMONN: Love, hate. Please. This is about reality, about life.

ALEX: It doesn't have to be.

EAMONN: Oh yes it does!

ALEX: Is that how you want to live, Connor? All your life, not trusting anyone.

EAMONN: It's better than living like you do, sitting alone, desperately waiting for someone to come back to you, knowing they detest you but pretending they don't.

ALEX: Hoping isn't the same as pretending.

EAMONN: Hoping, pretending, it's

ALEX: My life's sad but it's not that pathetic.

EAMONN: Isn't it? Even Connor who has fuck all in this life, hates you now.

CONNOR: Why'd you tell me to come here at exactly 11.20? What was the something you had to tell me that was so important?

ALEX: *(To himself.)* Jesus, he even knew it would only take twenty minutes to break me down.

EAMONN: So that you can see for yourself that in this life there is only one person you can trust. And that is you. No-one else. That's the real world. That's reality. Fin has learnt it. He's totally independent now. Alone, reliant on no-one but himself.

ALEX: Alone. Living in a hostel, alone. That's what you want for Connor? Don't trust anyone, don't rely on anyone.

EAMONN: If he learns that, he'll have learnt everything worth knowing. Everything he needs to cope in this bastard world.

ALEX: So now he really has hit rock bottom. He hates you, hates me, won't come to me when he needs someone. How's that going to help him? He's a young boy, immature, how's he going to cope?

CONNOR: What is the something so important that you had to tell me?

EAMONN: I'm gonna give you another chance.

CONNOR: What chance?

EAMONN: You can come home, Connor.

CONNOR: Really?

ALEX: There are conditions, Connor. Ask about the conditions.

EAMONN: Why do you think there'd be conditions?

ALEX: Because I know you.

EAMONN: No conditions. But to make sure it works, you have to cut off all ties with everyone you know. And we'll start again. Go to college, get cleaned up, get help to clean yourself, to get yourself off booze, an internship with my company when you finish college. And bingo, you've got yourself a future. What are you offering, Alex?

ALEX: Friendship. A place to come to from time to time. And love.

EAMONN: Well, I don't want to be sarcastic but it doesn't seem like much of a choice. It's like comparing a round the world holiday on a cruise ship with a tent in Skegness for a wet May bank holiday .

ALEX: Except that yours comes with you.

EAMONN: And my position, my values, my money and background, my contacts, my status.

ALEX: He had all of that since he was five. Look where it got him.

EAMONN: I've grown up too.

ALEX: Have you?

CONNOR: Will you both stop it! I'm here you know. I feel as if I'm the rubbish run down broken car that's sitting in the corner of the auction house. Nobody really wants it, but some think they might be able to do something with it. It's not much good, tires flat, engines worn through, colours gone, but, y'know, maybe with a bit of money spent on it, it might be a decent run-around for a year or so. And then what? What you gonna do with me then? When you see I'm still me. This is me. This is the person I am. What you gonna do then? Throw me out again? I'm never gonna be what you want. You want a little you, a little despicable me, a clone, a copy. I'm not you. In any way. And you know what, Dad? I never ever want to be you. Fin might have. But not me. In fact I'd go so far as to say, I want to be everything you're not.

ALEX: Ha!

CONNOR: And I don't want to be you either, Alex. Yes, you're kind and good. But I wouldn't want to be the sort of person who ends up pissing his life away because of someone else. You are pathetic, actually. You think you're not. But you are. I don't need either of you. I know my life is shit at the moment. It's no bloody fun to beg and sleep rough. But, I'm actually doing good to one person. One person who needs me. And soon, when or if she doesn't need me, or I don't want to be needed so much, I'm gonna move on. But there's a world out there. And I want to be part of it. There's things I can do. I don't know yet what they are and how to get them. But I'm young. And that's where I'm luckier than you, because I've got my whole life ahead of me. And you, well, what are you gonna do with your lives? Try and do something with them, will you?

Exits.

EAMONN and ALEX look at him as he leaves.

Black.

THE MITFORDS

Thanks to Felicity Dean and Jake Murray for help
developing early drafts.

Characters

UNITY

JESSICA

NANCY

DIANA

The Mitfords was first performed at Rialto Theatre, Brighton on 14 November 2017 with the following cast:

Heather Long   UNITY
                             JESSICA
                             NANCY
                             DIANA

Director   John Burrows
Production Manager   Paul Debreczeny
Stage Manager   Charlie Tipler
Tour Manager   Chris Taylor

UNITY: His eyes are so, it's expressive, you know. You know that feeling you get when you look into someone's eyes, and you know them, you connect with them. They're warm. They're deep and fluid. You know what I mean by fluid, don't you, moving around inside their, boundary, their black round bit. What do you call that bit, it sort of provides a boundary to all that's going on inside. And what's inside is all this love, this warmth, this beauty.

He's asked me to sit with him. I can't believe it. I've been at the restaurant for weeks, months, hoping he'd, well I know when he's there, you see. I know his movements. It's a small town, relatively, and it's known where he's going to be. So I sit there, for hours sometimes. I take someone with me, so I won't be, well, you're a bit of a loner, a nobody, if you sit there all by yourself, week in week out. I take a book of course if someone isn't there with me. Well, I always have a book anyway because I sit longer than anyone has the patience to, because sometimes he comes in much later. Never alone, he's always with a group, and they sit and talk. In his special place with a sort of screen around them. But it doesn't stop him from noticing me, particularly if I talk loudly and drop my book conspicuously and, you know, make myself known. I learnt to make myself noticed. I had to, didn't I, with you lot.

NANCY: Of course darling Unity. At least you didn't send your pet rat, what was his name, Ratula, how could I forget! Or that sweet little darling snake you used to put round the toilet chain to frighten one of your countless governesses. Thank God I'd long gone from the horrid nursery and schoolroom by the time you got there.

UNITY: You can't believe his smile. It enraptures you, engulfs you, takes you into his, orbit. Please don't say I'm being dramatic, Nancy. It's true. You know it. We've all felt it.

NANCY: Darling Unity, you're not being dramatic. You just always liked to shock. Remember the postmistress in Swinbrook was horrified when you lifted your skirt and, no knickers! What a hoot!

UNITY: And when he looks at you, it's as if you're the only one in the whole world. The only one he's interested in, cares about. Even Farve feels it. And remember what he's always said about him. Until he met him, that is.

NANCY: Even Tom. He got into quite a frenzy when he met him. Mark you, our little bro Tom was always rather prone to crushes, that sort of, well he had the tendency, didn't he? I mean half the boys in Eton …

Debo says you get rather transformed when you're with him, Unity. You shook when you were going up the stairs to see him. You could hardly walk. And she said she had to drink your cup of hot chocolate because your hands wouldn't stop shaking. And then Muv asked him if he had any good recipes for bread. It's killing!

UNITY: I'm aware that he keeps his eyes on me, all the time, even with all of you there. Even with Diana, and she's always been the Beauty.

NANCY: Oh darling, you're hardly ugly. Big! Big feet. Big hands. Huge hands. My god, those hands, they're colossal. But you aren't ugly. You just terribly, don't care very much. What you wear. How you look. Apart from your make up, the lipstick. But then he doesn't exactly appreciate lipstick, does he. I adore fashion. Oh darling Diana, that gorgeous Dior dress they're making me. And the Lanvin one. They're heaven. Backless. Mind you, I'm planning to wear it to Chatsworth to visit Debo but I'm sure I'll freeze to death! They will insist on not putting the heat up too much for fear of cracking all those 'works of virtue'.

UNITY: Virtuous. Honest. Such integrity. The first time we speak, he salutes me. You know how he does it, with his arm, like this. He does it to me. We talk. His friends look at me, wondering why he's talking to this young English girl. I tell him my middle name is Valkyrie, and that I was conceived in a little mining town in Canada called, ha, he laughs,' what! Swastika. Unglaublich! It means you are meant to be here, with us'.

'Have you ever been to a Wagner festival in Beyreuth?' he asks. No, I say. But I'd like to. And he turns to the other men watching me at the table and says, 'Don't forget that, Junge!'

NANCY: Muv threatens to throw me out the car just because I say something bad about him. 'If you've got nothing nice to say, you'd better get out!' Can you imagine! And we're driving to Inch Kenneth, in the middle of bloody nowhere! What a hoot!

UNITY: I want to be the power behind the throne. I always have, since I was little.

NANCY: Oh darling Unity, you were never little. You were always enormous. You towered over everyone. You had to be right at the back as a deb in your white gown and ostrich feathers. And there you were with old Ratula, which you managed to let go amongst all those debs. How we roared!

UNITY: In the restaurant I float towards him, but he doesn't stand, which is strange because he always does. His eyes are yellow round the edges, and I realise he's in the most terrible pain. I almost cry out. I want to soothe him, to kiss his adorable head, his glorious eyes, his sweet tender moustache. That day he puts his hand on my shoulder twice, and once on my arm. It was so exciting. Even you can feel that for me, Jessica.

JESSICA: I suppose it was exciting for you. Life was so dull. Wasn't it dull growing up? *I* always found it the dullest. None of you ever found it as dull as me. Maybe you, Unity, but for me it was as dull as …. It would be awfully dull were I to say ditchwater. As dull as a fish knife. I knew I would run away from it all. I opened up a running away account with Drummonds the bankers when I was twelve. They acknowledged receipt of my ten shillings and promised in a letter to be my obedient servants. That was exciting.

DIANA: It was because Muv and Farve wouldn't let you go to school, Jessica darling. I can't begin to understand why you should possibly have wanted to go to school. Horrid thought! They weren't the most wonderful parents but at least they did right there. And we had lovely moments as children. We had such fun. I have to say, it is rather typical of a communist to always hark on the negative side. Don't you remember the fun bits?

JESSICA: Diana, I'm still not talking to fascists. Address the others if you must.

I do remember that time with Pam during the General Strike in '26. All my family are on the side of the Tory bastards, making tea and sandwiches to help the scabs against the working classes. Pam is there early getting ready with the tea for the first shift of bus drivers. Suddenly, she feels someone outside, looking in. Hello, she says, what do you want? It's a fat old tramp, smelly, dirty. He has this great big belly and his clothes are torn and filthy. Quite disgusting. 'Any chance of a cuppa tea love?' Yes, one second, she says, fumbling around trying to get it done as quickly as possible. And as she does, he comes in. Wait outside my man, she says. But he comes in anyway and grabs her round her waist! 'Any chance of a kiss while we wait love'. She screeches and dashes out and as she does, she hears you Nancy squealing with laughter behind the disguise.

UNITY: I feel so sorry for him. Röhm is his oldest colleague and closest friend. Imagine having to do something like that to someone so close to you. It would be like me killing you, Jessica. Or you killing me. We said we would, if it came to it. Can you imagine what it must be like for him? He's had to arrest him himself you know. He's torn off his decorations. And when he went to arrest Heines, he found him in bed with a boy! What a shock for him. How dreadful to come across something like that. He doesn't like that sort of thing, you know. 'Shuft, du bist verhaftet!' 'Wretch, you are under lock and key.'

NANCY: Pam met him. He seemed very ordinary to her, like an old farmer in a brown suit. She didn't remember much more about him, what he said or what he did. But she remembered the new potatoes they ate.

UNITY: Of course <u>he</u> didn't kill Rohm you know. He's never killed anyone. And it's not true that he's a vegetarian. He loves sausages. Who said he's a vegetarian? You see what lies they say about him.

Sings Horst Wessel Lied

Sieg heil!

NANCY: I can't be bothered with all of that sort of thing. Far too boring. Where are the laughs? I'm reminded of the time I got myself a dear little flat in London. It was such fun, but I had to give it up after a few days. The floor of my bedroom was just a mass of underclothes. I could hardly walk through the room. Nanny did tick me off. Such a scream.

UNITY: I am walking along the Adolf Hitler Strasse and a little old lady, heavily burdened with bags, stops me and asks me the way to the station. I tell her go there, pointing in the wrong direction. Well, she shouldn't speak to Aryans. Not people like her.

JESSICA: Unity you are so vile! I am invited to go to Munich to see her. I think about it, how could I sneak in a gun, and shoot him. I don't quite know why I decide not to.

UNITY: Jessica, I'm not vile to my friends.

JESSICA: Oh really? What about you and your beloved Baumchen?

UNITY: Ahh Baumchen. We are kindred spirits. As soon as she sees my black shirt and my British Union of Fascists badge, which the Leader himself had given me, and I see das Hakenkreuz sitting firmly, proudly near her heart, we both know instantaneously that we will be great friends. In fact, it is she who first tells me that the *Führer* eats his lunch at Osteria Bavaria, the Ost, every Friday at about two. We talk for hours about Him and *'The iniquities of the Jewish race'*.

JESSICA: And then Baumchen's 'kindred spirit' whispers
in someone's ear that Baumchen in all her glorious and
virulent anti-semitism, might, just might, be Jewish herself.

UNITY: Well, it is my duty to say what I know to be true. We
are all his eyes and ears. He is just one man. He isn't able
to do everything. We are duty bound to be aware and to
bring criminal activity to book.

JESSICA: I have to get away. The Spanish Civil War is raging. I
want to get there, to help, to do something. This impossible
life of emptiness, of privilege, of boredom, while so close
to us those people are fighting, dying. And cousin Esmond
is out there, helping the plucky Republicans. I want to be
there too, at his side. They all say he's dreadful, a Red, a
nasty communist, even though he too is related to Winston.
In fact there's even gossip that he is actually Winston's
son. I see his picture on the back of his book. I stare and
stare at it. Oh, he's divine. Dark curly hair. His smile. I'm
already half in love with him, and haven't even met him.
He doesn't know me. How will I meet him! Then suddenly
I get an invitation to a relative we share. I wear a mauve
lame ankle length dress. I look in the mirror and think
of all those dark, beautiful girls in Spain he must know.
They're probably all thin too! Nevermind! We are seated
next to each other at the table. I want to go to Spain, I
whisper. Find an excuse and meet me outside after dinner,
he whispers back. We meet and we walk and we talk and
just like that, we fall in love.

DIANA: It's just like that with me and Oswald too.

JESSICA: Except Diana, you're already married. With two
children.

DIANA: Oh I adore him. As soon as I see him. I just fall
in love. Bryan's heaven. I adore Bryan. He's a darling
and he adores me beyond belief. We're the glamorous
couple. Everyone wants to be part of the Guinness set.
But once Oswald comes into my life, it's as if nothing else
is, worthwhile. Do you know what I mean, sweetheart?
Nothing has value away from this one man. He is literally

the world to me. Everyone is shocked that I can walk away from my life of riches, opulence, charm, beauty. And to what? To be a mistress of a married man. Not just social exclusion. Social suicide. 'You're destroying not only your life but that of your sisters. Who will want to marry them now!' Muv wails. And on top of it all, everybody loves Cimmie, Lady Cynthia Mosley, his wife, the mother of their three children, daughter of the Viceroy of India, Labour MP for Stoke-on-Trent. Thoroughly decent Cimmie. The man I crave is her first and only lover. And I am the reviled husband snatcher.

UNITY: He knows I can't bear Mussolini. I hate Italians. I'm having lunch with the Fuhrer in the Ost. Doctor Goebbels and various others are there too of course. They all set upon me because I say I don't like Il Duce, and he's coming tomorrow. Big thing for all of them, they're putting on such a show. It's all rather important because they want him on their side. But they really turn on me, bully me. I'm nearly in tears. Then the Fuhrer, puts his hand on my arm, supports me, not that he says anything against Musso, but he is so dreadfully sweet.

DIANA: We're all in Venice, Oswald, Cimmie, Bryan, me. A few others. I know the game. You don't make it obvious, you laugh and have a drink with the other woman, you whisper conspiratorially and chuckle at the idiocies of your respective husbands. Oh isn't he a dear old fool. I don't know what to do with him! You laugh and pretend her husband doesn't mean a thing to you. That you are barely aware of his existence. I know that's what I'm supposed to do. But it's not like that. We dance together, as close as can be. We sit right next to each other and whisper in each other's ears. We giggle and look at each other so that it actually becomes embarrassing for the others. We go off on our own without even making up excuses or going at different times. And we are unaware of it all. We are unaware of them. If we could stop for a minute and think about it, if we looked into the faces of our spouses, if we listened to the way others tutted, we would know. But that is another world. And the only world we are in, is the one populated by just the two of us.

UNITY: Muv met Him and I fear the whole experience was wasted on her. I had to translate and things get lost in translation. All she seemed to want to talk about is wholemeal bread. She doesn't feel his goodness and wonderfulness radiating out, like we do. Like you and me, Diana.

JESSICA: I have to make up an elaborate plan to run away without rousing any suspicions. If Muv or Farve get wind of it, they'll stop me. 'Try and get as much money as you possibly can', Esmond says. I have my running away account. It's got £50 in it. Esmond is impressed. I write to my obedient servants and arrange its withdrawal. I ask Muv to give me more money to buy clothes for our round the world trip which she is planning for me and Debo, to get me out of my state of depression. She's surprised that I seem so much brighter, and puts it down to our forthcoming cruise. She doesn't realise that my life is on the cusp of a revolution.

DIANA: We're dancing together. He's dressed in black, with his black eyes and black moustache. And me, all in white with my fair skin and blonde hair. What a sight it all is! But he won't leave Cimmie. She writes to him saying 'bloody, damnable cursed Ebury', the street where his flat is. 'How often does she come there?' And he writes back, dismissing her fears, using their own special cutesy language. He dismisses me to her, he includes me with other dalliances and talks of his 'frolicsome little ways'. He tells her she is the one for him, and that he will never leave her. Yet I have left Bryan and living with the boys in Eaton Square, a modest little house, and my whole entire life revolves around Oswald.

JESSICA: I pretend to Muv that I'm staying with friends in Dieppe for two weeks. That gives us two weeks grace before they realise I've fled the nest. We arrive in France and Esmond tells me, as he's already fallen in love with

me, and anyway we're going to marry eventually, there's
no reason to pay for two hotel rooms. We make love and
I come and I finally understand how boredom can truly
be alleviated. We're under age so can't marry immediately
without our parents' permission. We arrive in Spain and
by now the parents know I've disappeared, but they know
nothing else. They're worried I've been taken by white
slavers or joined a communist cell. When Farve hears the
truth, he slumps in a chair; 'worse than I thought!' He says.

We arrive in Bilbao after a three day voyage where every
last thing I had eaten over the past two weeks makes its
way back up my gullet. Esmond is a war correspondent
and we go out to be shown the fighting. The Hon Jessica
Mitford along with all those hardened war reporters. How
I wish I had been inclined to shoot with Farve when I was
offered the chance.

DIANA: I am watching the rally in London. They all look
glorious in their black shirts and black trousers. And
the most glorious of all is our glorious leader. They're
marching in the East End. Oswald won't let me be part of
it as much as I'd love to. He says those filthy Jews make it
too dangerous. There is certainly a great deal of shouting.

JESSICA: Unity has told Hitler that I have run away to Spain to
join the Reds. He said 'armes kind', poor child, apparently.

UNITY: How divine it is when you come to Munchen, Diana
darling. How I love being with you. We understand each
other so well. We go out together all the time. We meet up
with our friends, the storms. We are invited by the Fuhrer.
We travel, we are feted. We go to the raliies and have seats
right in the front. We travel there in a special Mercedes,
paid for and organised by Him himself. We have the same
faith, the same values, beliefs. And we share other things.
Very special things *(Laughs.)*

NANCY: Darlings, I am feeling rather left out here! I seem to
be just listening rather than saying anything. I do think it's
my turn. And I am already starting to have great success
at this time, before the war. I mean all your stories are

just about other men. Whereas I am by now a novelist, respected, lauded, making money. All you talk about is sex!

UNITY: I am invited to his flat. We sit together in his living room. A fire is roaring and his dog is asleep at his feet. I sit very near him. We sip schnapps. I long for him to touch me, to kiss me. He asks me about them, about the storms. Of course he knows about me and all of them. He knows everything. He is told everything. I am worried. Will he be angry? 'Tell me all about it, all the details,' he says.

There is a change in light and tempo here. UNITY starts marching to the sounds of thousands marching, Nazi marching music, red and black swastikas displayed and the head of Hitler highlighted on the back.

UNITY stops in the middle, ties a band round her eyes. It all takes place as she speaks and is interwoven to reflect what she says. She puts her arms out sideways, as if she were on a crucifix and splays her legs out wide. Music changes to Nazi songs, such as Hitler is our saviour etc. It can be an amalgamation of songs going from slow to fast to simulate the sexual act. As this happens, UNITY simulates sex with lots of different SS men until she and the music climax.

Your picture looks down, observes, throughout it all. I am blindfolded so that I can imagine it is you rather than all the others. The loud music is blaring in the background throughout. And the men, one after the other, one after the other. And the images that go through my mind while they are inside me, the thousands of feet marching in step. You, speaking to your masses, You, shouting, demanding, declaiming, all those thousands of people, yelling, screaming, adoring, You. Heil Hitler, Heil Hitler, Heil Hitler!

'Armes kind', poor child, he says, stroking my arm.

NANCY: It's all sexual, darling. What do you think all that hysterical speech making is, that feverish, over excited frenzy of his, if not one glorious come. Unity doesn't have a political bone in her body. You know that. It's just one big joke to her, running around in that big Mercedes, being Hitler's special friend. Carrying a gun. It's all a joke.

UNITY: I want Him to know how much I support Him. I'm going to let the world know. I write to Der Stürmer.

Dear Stürmer. As a British woman Fascist, I should like to express my admiration for you. I have lived in Munich for a year and read Der Stürmer every week. If only we had such a newspaper in England! The English have no notion of the Jewish danger. English Jews are always described as 'decent'. Perhaps the Jews in England are more clever with their propaganda than in other countries. I cannot tell but it is a certain fact that our struggle is very hard. Our worst Jews work only behind the scenes. They never come into the open, and therefore we cannot show them to the British public in their true dreadfulness. We hope, however, that you will see that we will soon win against the world enemy, in spite of all his cunning. We think with joy of the day when we will be able to say with might and authority: England for the English! Out with the Jews! With German greeting, Heil Hitler! Unity Mitford. PS: If you find room in your newspaper for this letter, please publish my name in full. I want everyone to know that I am a Jew hater.

JESSICA: That editor is a filthy butcher.

DIANA: But Jessica darling. Streicher's a kitten.

UNITY: I had a gorgeous time with Him. He was heavenly, in his best mood and very gay. He spoke a lot about Jews which was lovely.

JESSICA: When we were little, we had a divide down the middle of our bedroom. On Unity's side was Hitler and the swastikas. On my side was Lenin and the hammer and sickle. We had our own secret language and we were the very best of friends. I hate who you are Unity, but I love you in spite of it all.

UNITY: I hate communists as much as you hate fascists Jessica, though I have to say, I prefer to call myself a National Socialist. We may be political enemies, but that doesn't mean we shouldn't be personal friends. Of course I know Esmond wouldn't hesitate to shoot me for his cause, but then again, I wouldn't hesitate to shoot him. But that shouldn't affect us.

NANCY: I've had another book published. What a hoot! All this attention, and money. Of course that appalling man I'm married to insists on using up all my money. It really is just too dreadful. I tell him to leave but why should he when he has his cake and eats it too. I don't quite understand why I don't insist. It does seem a ridiculous imposition on me.

UNITY: I call him Wolfie now. He's so interested in history, you know, and very much our English history, too. I tell him about that story of William of Orange, you know the one where the first city he took was Exeter, and about how he rode into the city on a white horse with two hundred black men forming a guard of honour. It reminds me exactly of Reichsmarschall Göring, I say to him. He roars with laughter and says, 'Your sense of humour! You find everything funny, even Reichsmarschall Göring and niggers'.

He wants me to see a flat which he thinks will suit me perfectly. Oh gosh, it is heaven, so central, really big, rather grand. The couple who used to live there are standing together, holding each other. I don't want this sofa, I say. It'll have to go. The couple sniffle and sob.

DIANA: I'm running up the stairs to Unity's flat. What a surprise she'll have. Darling, I'll say. I got here sooner than I thought. As I walk in, I hear the sounds of Reichs music, there are men standing around her room and she is lying on the bed, oh, *(laughs)* you know the rest. I stand and watch. Once the storms leave, we sit and roar!

UNITY: He is exhausted when he comes back home after a party rally. He can't even talk. So we sit together listening to Wagner's Ride of the Valkyries from Bayreuth. We are in a trance, a trance of pure ecstasy.

I have seen Wolfie a lot lately which has been heaven. But now he has gone back to his mountain. To her. Apparently she is very jealous of me and has tried to commit suicide. Unsuccessfully I might add.

DIANA: Cimmie has died! Oh God. Do I really sound victorious. I don't mean it. Oswald is distraught. Everyone is horrified. She died of peritonitis. They had a dreadful row about me. Oswald stormed out and Cimmie spent the night crying and wrote to him in the morning apologising for her unreasonable behaviour. She said she'd been feeling dreadfully ill with awful tummy and back pain. She was rushed to hospital with a perforated appendix and later died of this awful infection. The doctor said she didn't lift a mental or physical finger to help herself live. She was thirty three. Of course that makes me the perfect monster. Oswald is so upset, he's rushed off on a European trip with Cimmie's sister, Baba. Oh I do think I shall die!

UNITY: We speak of what might happen if our two countries were at war. I know what I will do. I will simply kill myself. I will not be able to live if the two countries I love go to war. Wolfie gives me a gun. A little pearl handled pistol. He knows that I will use it to kill myself.

JESSICA: The family has gone wild. They're threatening all sorts of things, ward of court, all manner of hysteria. They go to Winston who appears to have bigger things on his mind! Esmond is sent a telegram from our family solicitors; 'Miss Jessica Mitford is a ward of court stop if you marry her without leave of judge you will be liable to imprisonment'. I get letters from the family. Nanny writes a frantic letter worried whether I have enough underclothes. Anthony Eden agrees to allow Nancy and husband Peter to get a lift aboard a naval destroyer on its way to Spain. I agree to go to see them. Esmond says not to trust any of you, the whole family are Nazis, he says. Not Nancy I say. Nancy will be on my side through thick and thin. Oh Nancy, you stand there so tall and beautiful, and you wave your blue kid gloves at us.

NANCY: I don't want you to make the same mistake I made and Diana made. Marry in haste, and look what happens.

I want you to do things properly. It's not respectable and society can make things pretty beastly to those who disregard its rules.

JESSICA: You've sided with the grown ups this time, haven't you Nancy. 'Come on board,' you say. Esmond has warned me. 'On no account must you get on the destroyer. ' You call out to me, 'There's roast chicken and creamed potatoes and carrots and peas and lashings of gravy.' I am so hungry. I can smell the gravy, taste its texture. But I stay firm.

Stalemate. Esmond manages to get a job as a correspondent, well more like translating Falange broadcasts into English for Reuters. He can't actually understand the language, but that doesn't stop him. Muv comes and is quiet and gentle and laughs a lot. Esmond grudgingly likes her. She and Farve agree to let us marry. It is the better of two dreadful options as far as they're concerned. Being pregnant probably helped their decision.

DIANA: How I hate Baba Metcalfe! Oswald is still travelling through Europe with her, mourning their loss, but that doesn't stop them having a torrid love affair, even though she is his sister-in-law. I am distraught.

JESSICA: We've come back to England and are looking for a house to rent in Rotherhithe. I am desperate for a cup of tea and approach a burly working man in the street. Can you be absolutely sweet and tell me where I can find a delicious cup of tea. He stares at me askance.

We find a darling little house to rent. It's tall and thin and links two warehouses along the Thames. We're utterly free. We have no constraints, no restrictions. We can do what we want. We have very little so when we're invited to the homes of the rich, we take what we want, fill our pockets. I don't know why Esmond stopped me cutting some curtains in one mansion to take home for our little place. We could use them far more than they could and they have so much to spare.

Housework is, well, such a hoot. After spending hours sweeping the stairs, I now understand that one must start at the top and move down. And my earlier method of soaping, rinsing and drying each article of crockery individually has now been replaced by the assembly line approach. It certainly takes up less time.

DIANA: Can you believe where Jessica is living with that awful Red. In Rotherhithe! It's an absolute slum. It's positively embarrassing. One of our friends wanted to go and see her but was worried about going into the slums and wore her oldest clothes. Jessica wrote to her afterwards and said, 'not to worry as your best clothes look like other people's oldest'. She can be sharp and rather bitchy, if you ask me. Has no appreciation any more of being part of society. Well she isn't. Not married to that Red. She's pregnant, mark you. Fancy bringing up a child in Rotherhithe!

JESSICA: Baby Julia has come into the world. She's glorious. We sit and watch her for hours, how she catches her feet and waves her divine arms about. The winter is vicious and Esmond won't let me accept Diana's presents of baby clothes. Muv is worried that she's too thin and says her legs are like Marlene Dietrich's. She cries a lot, but then all babies do. There's a measles epidemic and I take her to the clinic. She'll be fine, the nurse says. Breastfed babies get immunity to the disease from their mothers. I breastfeed her but have forgotten the implications of Muv's philosophy on health. The good body will heal itself, she always said. Which is fine if you have a cold. But not if you'd had no immunisations. The nurse wasn't to know. She is not to be blamed.

The day after she is buried, Esmond and I escape to Corsica. We find whatever money we can to get away from the horror... Oh God!

UNITY: Darling Jessica. I feel so desperate for your hurt.

JESSICA: Thank you, Unity.

DIANA: Oh glorious glorious day. Oswald and I are married! The Goebbels are hosting it at their flat. Darling Magda has arranged it all and it is perfectly heavenly. The Fuhrer is here too which makes it absolutely, what can I say, just too too marvellous. He looks in blooming health and his skin is peeling from sunburn. How I wish my sons could be here even for a moment, just to be blessed by a glimpse of him.

NANCY: Honestly, as if I am still just having fun. Nancy, she who only has fun! In the midst of all this dreadfulness, I travel to France to Perpignan to work with international charity organisations like the Red Cross to help the hundreds of thousands escaping Franco's vengeance. I work without stop, finding food, clothes, medication, accommodation for the refugees. Helping feed children under two, loading refugees onto ships, everyone crying for their Spain that they will never see again. Heartache, heartbreak.

I return to England as ardently anti-Nazi as Jessica. I write to Muv. 'If you could have a look, as I have, at some of the less agreeable results of fascism in a country, I think you would be less anxious for the swastika to become a flag on which the sun never sets.'

JESSICA: Esmond and I return from Corsica. We can't breathe back in England. We are suffocating, struggling, desperate. We have to get away. We decide to go to America.

UNITY: I still love you Jessica. You are my dearest most beloved sister and friend. Why won't you speak to me anymore?

DIANA: So typical of a communist to be hard. I mean Jessica, you're just entirely self-centred. Entirely uninterested in your beloved Unity, what's happening to her. Vaguely interested in the shocking bits but unconcerned at how terribly exciting it is for her. She's achieving what she's really set out to do, to shock, to be noticed. But it all suddenly stops, doesn't it. It all becomes so much less fascinatingly gruesome. Just gruesome and vile really.

UNITY: I have received a message that there is a telegram for me at the British consulate. I walk there and collect it. The telegram tells me that this morning Britain declared war on Germany. I go home and write to Muv and Farve. 'I send my best love to you all and particularly to my Jessica. I hope you will see the Fuhrer often when the war is over.'

I go now to Gauleiter Wagner's office and ask him if I will
be interned as an enemy alien. He tells me no and offers
me some petrol for my car. Please, I say to him, if anything
happens to me, I want you to promise that I will be buried
here in Munchen with my signed photograph of the Fuhrer
and my Nazi party badge. I give him an envelope. I leave
quickly before he opens it.

I drive to the Englischer Garten. It's my favourite place in
Munchen, apart from the Osteria. I think of the secluded
little glade where I sunbathed naked in the past. But
I stop just inside the park, only a few yards from the
Koniginstrasse and close to the Haus du Kunst. I take my
pearl handled pistol Wolfie gave me. I put it to my temple,
and I pull the trigger.

NANCY: War has been declared and we have heard nothing
from Unity. In mid-September we hear on good authority
that she's in a concentration camp for Czech women. I
have to say, my initial response is, well, there you go. A
little bit of poetic justice, don't you know. But in October
we hear news. Unity has been ill but is now recovering in
hospital.

The tally then for Hitler's girls is; one successful suicide,
Geli, two unsuccessful suicides, Eva and Unity, and a final
successful one, Eva. He knew she would try and commit
suicide, he gave her the gun for God's sake. Why didn't
he give her a gun with a sufficiently large calibre to make
a success of it. A bullet stuck in the back of her skull.
Honestly!

UNITY: Such pain! Where is the nurse? Nurse! Give me
morphine. Help me please! Ahhhh, yes, that's better. I can
open my eyes now. My hands can unclench. I can let my teeth
hang open. It hurts so much when they touch each other.

Who is that old woman? Her eyes are yellow and deep
black rings go round them. Her face is an old palette. The
colours meld into each other, smears, smudges of bright
colour, sploshed willy nilly across her ugly old face.

A man is sitting next to my bed. He peers at me, concerned, horrified, disgusted. 'Armes kind,' he says. I am confronted by a blur of red. There is a smell that attacks my nostrils. It hurts my skin. 'I have brought you these red roses, my Valkyrie.'

Who is this man? What does he want from me? Nurse, don't go away. Stay close with your morphine, your syringe.

There are too many men in this room all dressed in the same colour, dark colour. They talk, they shush each other. They look at me and shake their heads. They tut. They all bring flowers, chocolates. I don't want chocolates. I can't use my teeth, they will not work. Only morphine, directly into my veins, please Nurse.

The man looks into my eyes. Can he find them through all that colour? 'What do you want to do, my Valkyrie?' 'I want to go home', I murmur through the swirls in front of me.

The room is empty. The sun streams in. It hurts my skin. I hear footsteps running up the stairs. The door bursts open and there is a woman, and a young girl. They come too close. I feel water attacking my face, but all it is, is a single tear. 'Darling Unity,' I hear. It is Debo. Where is my Jessica, I think.

I will have some salt, I say. 'Do you mean tea, Unity?' Yes. All my words that come out are different to the ones inside me. They look perplexed. Don't you understand I mean tea! How can you be so stupid!

My head! My head!

They put me in a wheelchair and push me away from my nurses, into a train. Badump, badump, badump it goes, knocking each time on my teeth. The train stops and starts and shrieks and bellows. Muv gently finds a vein and I lie back listening to the muffled sounds of the world as we pass on our way through the war to England.

In Calais, hundreds of people are calling, Unity, Unity, is it true, did you, were you, I cover my face with my hands, with the rug as they carry me into an ambulance. Farve tries to protect me. Debo shields me. But still they call, lights flashing, Miss Mitford, is it true, did Hitler.....

JESSICA: What gets me rigid is the fact that here is a woman who not only was a friend of Hitler's but, to all accounts, told him all sorts of things that was of value to him about England, the Duke of Windsor, other royalty, aristocracy. Incited anti-Jewish sentiment, was a fervent supporter of the state's enemy, and had access to the entire upper echelon of Nazi power. And yet, she arrives back in England and is never interrogated, nevermind interrogated, she is never even questioned, she is never interviewed by anyone associated with the intelligence service in Britain. She isn't even invited to take a cup of tea. That's what England is. A quiet word, a small entreaty. It's who you're related to, who you can speak to.

DIANA: Anyway, look, I've got my own troubles. Many of which might have been avoided had my own flesh and blood not betray...

NANCY: Oh don't you dare round on me, Diana. It's the times. I'm working desperately hard to support the war effort. What? I mustn't let the authorities know that you've been travelling to Germany so many times, that you too were a great supporter and friend of Hitler's. Why not? Because you're my sister! We are at war! Our whole country, our lives, are in desperate danger.

DIANA: The head of MI5 calls me 'an extremely dangerous and sinister young woman' and says I should be 'detained at the earliest possible moment.' Max my baby is eleven weeks old. He's still breastfeeding. Have you ever experienced the agony of having to stop breastfeeding instantaneously. The pain endures for a week.

NANCY: Darlings. I have to tell you something. I now understand what you mean when you talk about love. After all this time, all these years, Hamish the homosexual fiancé, Peter the unfaithful wastrel of a husband. I'm now head over heels in love with Colonel Gaston Palewski. He's utter heaven. I adore him.

DIANA: I'm incarcerated in Holloway prison. Rule 18B, it's called. The Emergency Powers Act. Can you imagine? Me! You'd think they'd treat me well, a Lady, after all. But they push me around, they throw me into a basement room where the one single window is covered with sandbags. It is dirty, it is smelly, oh lord, smelly doesn't go half way to describing the stench, the unbearable fetid, putrid, rancid smell of that miserable little cell. On the bare damp floor is a small thin mattress. I am given a little blanket and even though it is midsummer, I am freezing cold. I understand where part of the smell comes from when the food arrives. It is inedible and the tea is cold. I have never felt quite so wretched. Thank the Lord Pam looks after the babies. That is, the nanny does. She is happy to have the thanks, the accolades, thank goodness for good old Pamela. But she doesn't have much to do with them. They don't get in the way of the chickens or the horses. Life goes on pretty much the same as before. Though there is a war on and she finds it really rather dreadful.

My dearest Oswald is in prison too. And we are not together. That is the hardest of all.

JESSICA: I'm sorry. I refuse to feel anything for fascists who have been given their just deserts. Quite bloody right! Let her rot in jail. Esmond and I are having a marvellous time in America. We're arranging meetings with everyone who can help us and doing all sorts of jobs to make a living. It is bliss and happiness underscores everything we do. Esmond says he will return to fight the Nazis as soon as necessary. Thank goodness it hasn't happened yet.

DIANA: I long for Oswald. I have heard he is not well and suffers terribly. I am moved to a larger cell, six by nine feet. I have a little bed and chipped basin. There are other prisoners around including a Jewish woman who was in Dachau. Holloway is dirtier than Dachau, she says.

A bomb has fallen and hit a main sewer on the ground floor. The prison is awash with urine and the toilets are overflowing. We haven't been able to wash for three days.

We're all ill with food poisoning. At least they don't lock the doors now when there is an air raid siren and we are able to huddle together and talk. We talk of our babies and of our husbands. It can't be long now before they let me go.

I receive letters from my beloved. He has grown a beard and it is red! He is able to study in Brixton, to read and learn languages. He writes 'my precious darling' and 'my darlingest one'. He tells me constantly how much he loves me.

UNITY: I am in Inch Kenneth. It is very quiet and nobody's around. I lie in bed, or sit in my chair. I no longer have a need to move, to do. Those feelings that made me run, talk, go, have all gone. I sit. I lie. Muv is constantly haranguing me. Everyone says Muv is an angel.

I look in the mirror and see myself. The colours have worn away, disappeared into my skin. They have left a sallowness with blotches of red. I recognise myself. I know who I am. Why do the others not see me?

I sit and wait for the war to end so the Fuhrer will come and visit me here in Inch Kenneth. He will so love the quiet and peace. We will drink schnapps and I will make him scones.

They say I look well, I look better, the swellings gone, I look just like my old self. Why do they say that? Why do they say anything? Why don't they just shut up! Oh shut up Muv. Will you just leave me alone! I eat and eat. And eat.

JESSICA: This is just to let you know that I have given birth to a gorgeous little girl. We call her The Donk, as she is a veritable little dinky-donk. I think she'll be known as Dinky.

DIANA: I long for my babies. I try to remember what they look like and have only one little photo to pore over. But Max was only eleven weeks and now he is over a year.

JESSICA: Esmond has joined the Canadian Royal Air Force. He has gone to war. We have been together for so long, day in day out. Now he's gone, it's as if I am walking around with just my left side. A whole portion of my body has just faded away. It makes everything dreadfully hard.

NANCY: It's so desperately difficult to get decent clothes nowadays, I have to be inventive. I have a little Queen Alexandra hat with feathers on the brim and I pull it down over my eyes. The Colonel says I look debonair. He loves being with me. He laughs and calls me a great wit. I know he loves being with me. I know he doesn't love it as much as I love it though. I tell him, I love you, Colonel. And he says, that's awfully kind of you.

UNITY: Muv! You've put your bloody knitting on my chair. You are such a bloody fool! That's my chair. Why don't you just bloody get out of this house. Just leave me alone. I don't want any of you. Go away!

What is that, over there, out the window. Who's coming? It's a man. It's him. He's come to get me, to take me away, to take me with him. To be by his side. Wolfie? Is it you? Have you come for me at long last? I've been waiting and waiting, and, wait, it's, there's a light around him, encircling him, see, he's not wearing a grey uniform, a black uniform, there is no moustache. He's wearing a white cloak, his hair is long, and he has a sweet, smile, he's smiling directly at me.

DIANA: My boy has been rushed into hospital for an appendectomy. I am not allowed to go there, to be at his side. I am here, within these dreadful walls, stuck, alone, not even with Oswald to give me strength. I pace and pace, all night long. I think of Cimmie. I'm so sorry Cimmie. I'm so sorry you weren't able to lift a mental or physical finger to help you live.

JESSICA: I've decided to go and live in England so that I can be near Esmond when he is on leave. I cable Esmond on 1st December; 'Leaving Friday. So terrifically excited'. On 2nd December I receive a cable in return from Esmond. Excitedly I tear it open. It doesn't make sense. Why would he write this? I read it again and again. The words are a jumble. 'Regret to inform that your husband Pilot Officer Esmond Mark David Romilly missing on active service

November 30.' Why is Esmond using all his names? What does he mean by this?

UNITY: Oh God in heaven, hallowed be thy name. Thy kingdom come. Thy will be done. Why have Thou willed my Jessica to suffer so much? Why did you let her husband die? It must be because they are both communists which is against thy will. Oh Lord I am your servant. You are my guide, my leader. I am yours. Thine. *(Sings)* Onward Christian soldiers, marching as to war. With the cross of Jesus

Our brother Tom has been killed. I am very sad. Why is everyone dying, Lord?

DIANA: All the British Union of Fascist women have been released. Apart from me. There is still no charge against me. The newspapers call me the most hated woman in England. Winston has sent a memo to Herbert Morrison asking why Rule 18B prisoners aren't able to have daily baths. He has been told this is one of the hardships I mind the most. They summon me to tell me I can have a bath every day. That would be splendid news if I didn't know that there are only two degraded bathrooms in the wing and enough water for four baths for all the women. We take it in turn and have roughly one bath a week. They interrogate me and ask me about Hitler and I tell them we have always been for peace.

Eighteen months have passed since I have been with my husband or my children. But today I hear that I am to be reunited with Oswald. We will be interned together. Oh happy day. Happy, happy day!

The prison Oswald and I are living in is a deserted cotton mill. It's austere and dingy and there is a sadness that drapes round it. But inside we laugh and we love. We grow vegetables and we have an old gramophone.

JESSICA: I can't believe they're releasing Diana and the fascist. Three years is not long enough for them. They should throw away the key.

UNITY: Muv hides the paper. She doesn't want me to see that my Fuhrer is dead. He died with her. They married, it says.

NANCY: I am living in Paris. I have followed the Colonel. I can't bear to be far from him. We see each other often and I try not to tear him apart when I see him with other women. I have become a lady of letters. I receive honours, awards, marvellous reviews and critiques. And heaps and heaps of money. It's all rather a hoot!

UNITY: Jessica. The war is over. I am alone. All I have is God and our infuriating Muv. Why do you never contact me? Why won't you speak to me? The Lord has spoken to me and said I must forgive you and you must forgive me. We are sisters. Is there anything closer? I love you. Why won't you speak to me?

They say he was evil, that because of him six million Jews were killed. They call it a holocaust. I don't understand that word.

I see his gentleness, his kindness, the love that I feel when I look deep into his eyes. He smiles at me with just a twitch of his lips and a sparkle in his eyes. Valkyrie, he says. My English Valkyrie. Come. I am waiting for you.